CORPORATE CRIME IN CANADA

A Critical Analysis of Anti-Combines Legislation

Colin H. Goff
Dept. of Sociology   Northern Lights College

Charles E. Reasons
Dept. of Sociology   University of Calgary

PRENTICE-HALL OF CANADA, LTD., SCARBOROUGH, ONTARIO

Canadian Cataloguing in Publication Data

Reasons, Charles E., 1945-
  Corporate crime

Includes bibliographical references and index.
ISBN 0-13-173302-8

1. Antitrust law - Canada. 2. Commercial crimes -
Canada. I. Goff, Colin Harford, 1949-

II. Title.
KE1639.R42   343'.71'072   C77-001446-1

Prentice-Hall, Inc., Englewood Cliffs, New Jersey
Prentice-Hall of Australia, Pty., Ltd., Sydney
Prentice-Hall of India Pvt., Ltd., New Delhi
Prentice-Hall International, Inc., London
Prentice-Hall of Japan, Inc., Tokyo
Prentice-Hall of Southeast Asia (PTE.) Ltd., Singapore

Design: Julian Cleva

ISBN 0-13-173302-8

1 2 3 4 5 W 82 81 80 79 78

Printed and bound in Canada by Webcom Limited

Dedication

To Fran, Erv and the countless others who bear the brunt of corporate crime.

Table of Contents

Preface

Our purpose in writing this text is to examine an aspect of a sorely neglected topic—corporate crime. There is a great lack of material on this subject in Canada. While corporations are having ever increasing impact and control over our lives, we know little concerning their legal deportment. While much attention is being given to street crime and common criminals, we know practically nothing about suite crime and suite criminals. Hopefully this study will act as a catalyst for more thorough and penetrating analyses of the various forms and manifestations of "upperworld crime". We believe social scientists should study not only the poor and the powerless, but also the rich and powerful. From an analysis of the role of the rich and powerful in Canadian society we will gain a better understanding of their relationship to the poor and powerless.

Our intellectual debts are many and varied, including Karl Marx, Max Weber, E. A. Ross, E. H. Sutherland, Gil Geis, Richard Quinney, William Chambliss, Ralph Nader, C. Wright Mills, Ray Charles, Bill Yoels, Brian Gibbon, Sarah Haley, Rich Sullivan, and Lloyd Wong. We owe particular thanks to Jon Penman for his encouragement and two anonymous reviewers for their helpful comments. Professor Ben Carniol's patient and considered review of the final text was particularly helpful. In preparing the manuscript much useful assistance was given by Marilynne Mocan, Arna Reasons, Myra Phipps, Myrtle Murray and Marion Elaschuk.

Introduction

Before we can undertake a study of corporate crime in Canada the nature and scope of the term "suite" crime must be clarified. By "suite" crime we mean the illegal behaviour which occurs in the business suites of the corporate, professional and civic elites of society. Such crimes as misrepresentation of advertising, price fixing, fraudulent financial manipulations, illegal rebates, misappropriation of public funds, splitting fees, fraudulent damage claims, failure to maintain safety standards and the violation of human rights are examples of suite crimes. These types of offences are largely carried out by persons representing an organization and are committed for individual and/or collective benefits. But this definition of suite crime still leaves much to be explained regarding the scope and nature of such offences. These types of crimes do not include those "common crimes" which may occur in suites but are unrelated to role performance and/or organizational demands. For example, the murder of a corporate executive by another employee of the company may occur in the suites but would only come under the guise of suite crime if it was done as part of organizational needs and demands.

Hopefully our study will aid in further clarifying the nature and scope of suite crime. The need to study suite crime is due in part to the increasing power large organizations and professional elites have over the citizenry. The impersonality and apparent lack of accountability of corporations and their leaders increases the dehumanization and depersonalization of citizens confronted by corporate power. The investigation and clarification of the role of corporations upon citizen's lives and of the role of possible controls on corporations will hopefully lead to a reduction of feelings of powerlessness. Moreover, suite crime costs the public much more than street crime, while it also entails physical injuries and even death. Finally, the dictates of justice demand that suite crime and suite criminals be critically analyzed and forcefully dealt with by the state. If equality in the law is to be more than a hollow phrase, the illegal behaviour of the rich and powerful should be scrutinized along with that of the poor and the powerless.

While the concept of "suite" crime is somewhat broad, and includes a variety of offences, we have selected anti-combines legislation as our major focus of study. Although dealing with only certain types of corporate crime, anti-combines legislation reflects dominant values which are the basis for other legislation purportedly controlling "suite" crimes. A major cornerstone of capitalist ideology has been free enterprise in a competitive marketplace. Anti-combines legislation is the major federal means of controlling corporations and their economic activity within our capitalist state; therefore, such laws symbolize the state's commitment to free enterprise and competition. Since the institutions of the state, including its laws, largely reflect dominant interests, a study of anti-combines legislation will provide insight into the actual purpose and effect of such laws compared with "public interest" statements. Also, since anti-combines laws have been on the books since 1889, they provide an excellent opportunity for the socio-historical analysis of the emergence of and changes in laws over a period of more than eighty years. Furthermore, archival data exist which cover the lengthy history of these laws and provide invaluable insight into their emergence and change. Finally, carrying out an in-depth analysis of this legislation precludes undertaking such a study of other types of suite crime.

The following chapters attempt to provide the reader with an initial understanding of the nature and scope of suite crime generally, and an in-depth analysis of anti-combines legislation specifically. From a general discussion of the issues and theories in the study of crime in Chapters one and two, the text moves into a specific analysis of the nature, origins, scope and effect of anti-combines legislation including possible alternatives to current policy. Each chapter provides a foundation for the next and collectively they provide a picture of an increasingly significant aspect of Canadian society which has been largely ignored.

Chapter 1 explores the differences between street and suite crimes. While most street crimes have easily identifiable victims and criminals, the victim-offender relationship in suite crime is less easily recognizable. Although violence is almost entirely associated with street crime, most crime in the streets is not violent while some suite crime entails violence. The significance of suite crime to the public is measured not only in terms of economics and physical well being, but also in terms of the justness of Canadian society. Misconceptions concerning both street and suite crimes detract from the proper understanding of both by the public.

The relative merit of various theories of crime to the study of corporate criminality is pursued in Chapter 2. Both "kinds of people" and "kinds of environment" theories of criminality have shortcomings when applied to the study of criminality generally, and suite crime specifically. The "power/conflict" approach to the study of crime is believed to be the most useful, integrating a theory of the emergence of laws with the analysis of their operation, both in the context of state interests. Using a conflict method of study, we can analyse state interests in both the emergence and administration of anti-combines legislation. While anti-combines legislation apparently contradicts the conflict perspective, an exploration of the law's origin and subsequent administration will reveal the extent to which it actually supports the conflict approach.

Chapter 3 provides an analysis of the emergence of anti-combines legislation within the context of "socio-political" events in late nineteenth century Canada. Although purportedly protecting the public interest, initial legislation was largely a product of business interests and concerns. An expressive law defining the rightness of free enterprise and competition, it had little effect upon illicit pursuits. The law's ineffectiveness is evident in few prosecutions and the general unenforcibility of its provisions. Anti-combines legislation appears to have emerged as a product of *popular unrest* and *economic crisis* and it apparently convinced certain segments of the public that something was being done.

The significance of the merger movement in the early 1900s and Mackenzie King's role in formulating and administering anti-combines policy are discussed in Chapter 4. While a significant number of mergers occurred during the first decade of this century, Mackenzie King failed to see that they were potentially harmful and needed to be investigated. In fact, King viewed big business as healthy, and pursued a hands-off policy concerning corporations and their activities.

Chapter 5 critically assesses legislative developments in anti-combines policy since World War II. The influence of business interests in shaping such legislation to their liking is readily apparent. In spite of recommendations for a tougher policy regarding combines violations, subsequent legislation has been relatively innocuous. The significance of dominant economic interests is particularly evident in recent proposed changes under Stage Two of the anti-combines revisions, and in the make-up and proceedings of the Bryce Commission concerning Corporate Concentration.

Chapter 6 provides a statistical analysis of violations of the anti-combines Act by Canadian corporations. These data suggest that many corporations are recidivists and that the largest corporations in Canada are relatively immune from the law when compared to their smaller counterparts. Furthermore, intercorporate crime is evident but has largely been ignored by the government. Thus, those corporations that are the largest and most powerful are least likely to feel the brunt of government investigation and prosecution. Our data suggest that the government might better direct its efforts to more prestigious and potentially more criminal organizations.

The organization and emphasis of anti-combines enforcement policy is further explored in Chapter 7. Three aspects of enforcement are analyzed: the actual enforcement records, 1889-1972; the number of mergers and prosecutions of them by government, as well as an analysis of their economic concentration in various industrial sectors; and the amount of financial assistance to and the number of employees in the Combines Branch. The record of actual punishment of corporations is appalling, with no one ever imprisoned for offences against the anti-combines Act and most offenders receiving relatively minor fines and orders of prohibition. Although mergers have greatly increased in the last two decades, investigation and prosecution has been almost totally absent. Finally, proportionately small amounts are spent on policing this vital aspects of Canadian society. The data on the three aspects of enforcement which we explore suggest that the government has a great deal to do if we are to take seriously the stated aims of anti-combines legislation.

Chapter 8 discusses possible policy changes in light of the findings of previous chapters. Both individuals and corporations may be held liable for anti-combines violations. Given the rational, well-organized and premeditated nature of such offences, combinations of heavier policing, increased fines, imprisonment, public exposure and corporate restraint or dissolution may act as deterrents to such behaviour. Class action suits in particular may provide a vehicle for greater public vigilance and action against such suite crime. Furthermore, community control through local consumer councils may provide a potential means of addressing the problem.

Such remedies to the problem of combines violations are reformist in nature, and assume we can effectively address the problem through specific changes in social control. However, in a society which stresses the importance of competition, success and material wealth, the emphasis placed on such values contributes to *both* legal and illegal behaviour. In a capitalist society where the accumulation of wealth is of paramount importance, corporations may attempt to achieve that goal through any means available. In fact, some suggest that concentration and monopoly are inevitable and necessary in our capitalist society. One implication of this approach is the advocacy of an alternative socio-economic system. Of course, if concentration and monopoly are inherent in our economic system one might advocate the elimination of anti-combines laws since they are out of step with the needs of the state. Both of these extreme proposals are possible alternatives to current practices; they radically change the assumed relationship of corporations to the state, laws and ultimately the public.

As is inevitable in any study of society, our personal views and perspectives have influenced our analysis. While they cannot be eliminated through a ritualized appeal to objectivity, their impact can be minimized by a frank acknowledgement of them. Our interest in suite crime is largely based upon our belief that we have a double standard of justice, i.e., one for the rich and one for the poor. We believe that most students of crime in Canadian society have in the past and continue today to perpetrate a distorted image of most crime as violent street crime. Furthermore, we believe suite crime is more detrimental to our society not only in terms of economic loss, but also in terms of cherished values and physical and psychological well-being. Our personal experiences and professional training have largely contributed to our use of the conflict perspective rather than the order approach. Also, we feel the government is implicated in a benign neglect of the interests of most consumers while solidly supporting the Canadian corporate elite. We believe that meaningful attempts to resolve these problems will come primarily from the collective efforts of consumers and other peoples' collectives which oppose and attempt to change the emphasis of government. Finally, it is our feeling that social scientists have an obligation not only to critically assess dominant institutions, but to suggest, where possible, alternative institutional forms.

CHG
CER

CHAPTER 1

Street and Suite Crime

"The thief who is in prison is not necessarily more dishonest than his fellows at large, but mostly one who, through ignorance or stupidity, steals in a way that is not customary. He snatches a loaf from the baker's counter and is promptly run into gaol. Another man snatches bread from the table of hundreds of widows and orphans and similar credulous souls who do not know the ways of company promoters; and, as likely as not, he is run into Parliament."

George Bernard Shaw quoted in Gilbert Geis, "Upperworld Crime," in *Current Perspectives on Criminal Behavior*, ed. Abraham S. Blumberg (New York: Alfred A. Knopf, 1974), pp. 123-124.

A cursory look at national and local criminal statutes attests to the diversity of behaviours defined as criminal. For example, the Criminal Code of Canada includes in its definition of crime, offenses against public order (e.g., treason and other offenses against the Queen's authority and person, sedition, prize fights; offenses against the administration of law and justice (e.g., corruption and disobedience); sexual offenses, offenses against public morals and disorderly conduct (e.g., seduction of a female between 16 years and 18 years old, obscene materials, crime comics); disorderly houses, gaming and betting (e.g., common bawdy-house); offences against the person and/or reputation (e.g., homicide, venereal diseases, blasphemous libel, hate propaganda); offenses against rights of property (e.g., theft, robbery, extortion); fraudulent transactions relating to contracts and trade (e.g., fraud, breach of contract); wilful and forbidden acts in respect of certain property (e.g., arson, cruelty to animals); offenses relating to currency (e.g., counterfeiting, defacing or impairing); and attempts, conspiracies or accessories in these areas.[1]

So far we have used the word 'crime' in a broad sense. Like Humpty Dumpty I took it to mean what I meant it to be and yet I trust that we had a measure of mutual understanding. Already this is a miracle in human discourse that a word as colorful, diverse and rich in shadings as the word "crime" should convey to us any meaning at all. It is a tribute to the breadth of the human mind, but also to its craftiness and sleight of hand. This does not really get any better as one enters the process of definition and you are all too familiar with the double-dealing, buck-passing and circular reasoning that goes on. Nullum crisen sin lege is an old presumption and is still what most definitions come down to: crime is what the law says it is. This is no significant advance from Humpty Dumpty's argument because we are quite able to invent laws to fit what we want to call crime, although this is not often necessary (as in war crimes) since the fantastic elasticity of criminal laws covers pretty well all human behaviour, which for one reason or another becomes a problem to us, or at least to some of us.[2]

While in theory our freedom as citizens rests on the fact that no act is a crime unless so specified in law, in practice we have an enormous amount of behaviour defined as criminal in Canada, includ-

---

1 Minister of Justice, *Canada Criminal Code and Selected Statutes* (Ottawa: Information Canada, 1973).

2 J. W. Mohr, "Facts, Figures, Perceptions and Myths—Ways of Describing and Understanding Crime," *Canadian Journal of Criminology and Corrections,* 15 (July, 1972), p. 42.

ing over 700 Criminal Code sections, 20 000 federal offenses, and 30 000 provincial offenses which exclude municipal laws.[3] The sheer number of statutes is staggering to the imagination. A theory accounting for both the emergence and administration of laws within the context of the nation-state is crucial to understanding the nature of crime in our society and will be addressed in Chapter two.

Most students of crime, like most citizens, take the crime problem as given, with little argument regarding its nature or scope. The crime problem is assumed to be self-evident and its dimensions are hardly arguable.[4] This common conception of the crime problem is embodied in the term "street crime". When one talks about the crime problem, a common meaning is often assumed which emphasizes offenses against the person and particularly crimes of violence, e.g., robbery, assault, murder, rape. The imagery evoked by the concept "street crime" is one of dark shadows, dirty alleys and hordes of the criminally inclined lurking on public streets. "Street crime" has long been a rallying cry for "wars on crime" by politicians, police officials and other civic leaders. However, when one looks beyond the rhetoric of street crimes, one discovers that most murders, rapes and assaults are not committed in the streets, but in homes, taverns, automobiles and parks. Such a conception is even losing meaning regarding robbery. As one observer notes:

I will deal here mainly with street crime, and particularly robbery. In fact the phrase "street crime" is a misnomer, at least in New York. Most robberies now occur inside, in hallways, elevators, shops, or subways. You are safer out on the sidewalk.[5]

In actuality, most crimes in the streets are committed by vagrants, prostitutes, drunks, panhandlers, petty thieves and auto thieves. It would appear that to avoid murder, assault, rape or robbery, it might be advisable to stay away from home, family, friends and local drinking establishment and to spend time in the streets. Furthermore, violent crimes account for a very small proportion of the criminal behaviour in Canada. In Canada and the United States crimes of

---

3 Law Reform Commission, *Law*, 1976.

4 Since only the Federal Government can make criminal law, in the strictly legal meaning of the term only those acts legislated against in the Criminal Code of Canada are crimes. However, for most practical purposes the "offenses" found in provincial and municipal statutes are viewed as crimes and similar in their consequences. See Robert A. Silverman and James Teevan Jr. (eds.) *Crime in Canadian Society* (Toronto: Butterworth and Co. Ltd.) 1975, pp. 3-4.

5 Andrew Hacker "Getting Used to Mugging," *The New York Review of Books*, 20 (April 16, 1973), p. 9. Reprinted with permission from *The New York Review of Books*. Copyright © 1973 Nyrev, Inc.

violence account for less than 10% of all crime.[6] Table 1-1 shows that only about 6% of all offences in Canada are violent. While the rate of violent crime per 100 000 population increased between 1965-1974, so did the rate of nonviolent crimes which make up the bulk (over 90%) of crimes in Canada.[7] Thus, both the absolute number of crimes and the rate per 100 000 people have increased between 1965-1974.

TABLE 1-1.   CRIMES OF VIOLENCE AS A PERCENTAGE OF TOTAL
OFFENCES AND OF CRIMINAL CODE OFFENCES, CANADA,
1965-1974

			Violent Offences		
Year	*Total Offences No.**	*Criminal Code Offences No.*	*No.*	*% of Actual Offences*	*% of Criminal Code Offences*
1965	989 451	628 418	58 780	5.9	9.4
1966	1 094 889	702 809	69 386	6.3	9.9
1967	1 190 207	786 071	77 614	6.5	9.9
1968	1 335 444	897 530	87 544	6.6	9.8
1969	1 470 760	994 790	95 088	6.5	9.6
1970	1 574 145	1 109 988	102 361	6.5	9.2
1971	1 648 817	1 166 457	108 095	6.6	9.3
1972	1 653 316	1 192 891	110 468	6.7	9.3
1973	1 813 918	1 302 938	117 764	6.5	9.0
1974**	2 013 725	1 459 845	126 353	6.3	8.7
% Change					
1974/65	+ 103.5	+ 132.3	+ 115.0	—	—

*   Includes Criminal Code,
Federal Statute, Municipal
By-Law, and Provincial
Statute Offences

**   Preliminary figures

SOURCE:
Statistics Canada, Catalogue No. 85-205
Annual Publication of *Crime Statistics*
(Police) and Preliminary Bulletin, 1974.

PREPARED BY: Statistics Division,
Ministry Secretariat
August, 1975

6 See Statistics Canada, *Canada Year Book 1973* (Ottawa: Information Canada, 1973); Federal Bureau of Investigation, *Uniform Crime Reports—1974* (Washington, D.C.: U.S. Government Printing Office, 1975).

7 Canada's violent crime rate per 100 000 population remains about one fourth that of the United States between 1965-1974. See *Selected Aspects of Criminal Justice* (Ottawa: Ministry of the Solicitor General, March, 1976).

A great deal of attention is given to "street crime" and street criminals; however, relatively little attention is paid to "suite crime" and suite criminals. By "suite crime" we are referring to the illegal behaviour which occurs in the business suites of the corporate, professional and civil elites of society. Such crimes as misrepresentation of advertising, price fixing, fraudulent financial manipulations, illegal rebates, misappropriation of public funds, splitting fees, restraint of trade, failure to maintain safety standards and violation of human rights are examples of suite crimes. Evidence suggests that such "suite crimes" are as pervasive as "street crimes", if not more so, and result in a great deal more financial loss, while also entailing death and injury.[8] However, we have almost totally ignored such offenses in Canada. Data regarding street crime and street criminals are voluminous compared to available data on suite crime and suite criminals. The following news report is applicable to Canada.

White-collar crime is evidently costing billions of dollars more per year than violent or street crime in the United States, yet there is no comprehensive effort to keep track of it ... federal agencies concerned with crime are making few attempts to study white-collar crime, its magnitude or effects.[9]

Even less attention has been given to corporate crime in Canada than in the United States. One can count the studies of corporate crime on one's hand and crime control agencies do not appear to be eager to investigate this area. For example, the Solicitor General's priorities are almost solely limited to "common crimes" and "common criminals".[10]

Is Corporate Crime "Crime"?

Criminologist Edwin Sutherland noted some time ago that the criminality of corporations was like that of professional thieves in that corporations are persistent recidivists; their illegal behaviour is much more extensive than the prosecutions and complaints indicate; the businessmen who violate the laws designed to regulate business do not customarily lose status among their business associates; businessmen customarily feel and express contempt for law, for government, and for governmental personnel; corporate crime, like the professional

8 Richard Quinney, *Criminology: Analysis and Critique of Crime in America* (Boston: Little, Brown and Company, 1975), pp. 131-161.
9 "White Collar Crime Ignored," *The Calgary Herald*, May 28, 1975, p. 25.
10 *Guide Research Program 1976-77* (Ottawa: Solicitor General of Canada, 1976).

thief, is highly organized.[11] However, there are important distinctions between corporate criminality and that of the professional thief. The corporate criminal does not conceive of himself as a criminal and neither do most of the public because he does not fit the stereotype of the criminal. The professional thief views himself as a criminal and is viewed as such by the general public. While the professional thief has a "mouthpiece" (attorney) to argue against specific charges, corporations employ experts in law, public relations and advertising. Such corporate "mouthpieces" provide a much wider range of services than the "mouthpieces" of the professional thief do. Their duties include influencing the enactment and administration of the law, advising clients on how to break the law with relative impunity, defending in court those few clients who have the misfortune of being specifically charged and most importantly, building up and maintaining the corporation's status and image in the public's mind.

It is particularly those factors distinguishing the corporate criminal from the professional thief which help to maintain the appearance of non-criminality. The sharply dressed, neat appearing corporate executive who pays taxes, contributes to local charities and juvenile delinquency funds, and is an elder in the church, fails to match the stereotyped image of the criminal who, with premeditation, earns his livelihood through victimizing the public. If the mass media emphasized suite crime in the same manner it did street crime in an attempt to stress their similarities, there would likely be financial repercussions.

Nearly all the advertising revenues of the newspapers and mass magazines, as well as of radio and television stations and networks, come from these same corporations and their smaller counterparts . . . the newspapers have never despite recent sociological relevations ventured statistical summaries of the situation as they regularly do with lower-class, police-reported crimes—a marked case of class bias.[12]

Why do we tend to evaluate "street crime" so differently from "suite crime"? The direct, personal, face to face threat of physical violence is significant in "street crimes", i.e., murder, rape, assault, robbery. As one student of crime states:

I realize that muggers take much less from us than do corporate, syndicate and white-collar criminals. I have little doubt that the average executive swindles more on his taxes and expense account than the average addict steals in a typical year. Moreover, I am well aware that

---

11 E. H. Sutherland, *White Collar Crime* (New York: Holt, Rinehart & Winston, Inc., 1961).

12 Ferdinand Lundberg, *The Rich and the Super-Rich* Copyright © 1968 by Ferdinand Lundberg. Published by arrangement with Lyle Stuart.

concentrating on street crime provides yet another opportunity for picking on the poor, a campaign I have no wish to assist. It is a scandal that a bank embezzler gets six months while a hold-up man is hit with five years. Yet it is not entirely their disparate backgrounds that produce this discrimination.

A face to face threat of bodily harm or possibly violent death is so terrifying to most people that the $20 or so stolen in a typical mugging must be multiplied many times if comparisons with other offenses are to be made. I have a hunch that a majority of city dwellers would accept a bargain under which if they would not be mugged this year they would be willing to allow white-collar crime to take an extra ten percent of their incomes. Of course we are annoyed by corporate thievery that drives up prices, but the kind of dread included by thuggery has no dollar equivalent or, if it does, an extremely high one.[13]

While there is obvious physical danger and harm from some "street crimes" the belief that "suite crimes" are not violent is false.

Corporate crime kills and maims. It has been estimated for example, that each year 200 000 to 500 000 workers are needlessly exposed to toxic agents such as radioactive materials and poisonous chemicals because of corporate failure to obey safety laws. And many of the 2.5 million temporary and 250 000 permanent worker disabilities from industrial accidents each year are the result of managerial acts that represent culpable failure to adhere to established standards.[14]

However, when automobile accidents, airplane crashes or industrial disasters occur, culpability is usually found among those directly involved in the accident or disaster. In discussing the nearly 100 000 United States workers who die each year as a result of exposure to job health hazards, Swartz notes:

One of the more insidious tactics used by the corporate perpetrators of crime is to blame the victims for what happens to them. The National Safety Council, a corporation-funded institution, frequently runs "safety" campaigns. The point of these campaigns is always that the workers are careless and lazy, and do not take the measures necessary to protect themselves (wearing safety helmets, ear plugs, etc.). Never is the corporation held the culprit.[15]

13 Hacker, "Getting Used to Mugging," p. 9.
14 Gilbert Geis, "Deterring Corporate Crime," in *The Criminologist: Crime and the Criminal*, ed. Charles E. Reasons (Pacific Palisades, California: Goodyear Publishing Company, 1974), pp. 246-247.
15 Joel Swartz, "Silent Killers At Work," *Crime and Social Justice*, 3 (Summer, 1975), p. 19.

When alleged defects in manufactured products or violation of safety standards are investigated and substantiated, they are usually interpreted as quirks or accidents with possible civil, but not criminal, liability. In Quebec, about 45 construction workers die on the job each year while approximately 13 500 are injured. According to Réal Mireault, head of the Quebec Construction Office:

Employers should stop blaming accidents on workers and instead enforce safety regulations and give their employees safety training.[16]

Although persons might use the threat of violence in robbery, they will seldom employ it. Likewise, the probability of injuries and deaths from suite crime may be low related to the number of offenses. Nonetheless, both types of offenses periodically result in injury and death, but only street crimes bear the brunt of full prosecution. For example, mercury poisoning from the Dryden Chemical plant in Northwestern Ontario is evident among native people in the area, but it will not likely result in the laying of criminal charges. Such a decision is based largely upon legal conceptions of causation, intent and culpability, all of which mitigate corporate responsibility. Nonetheless, physical harm, injury and often death are the results of this disease. Whether death or injury occurs at the hands of an assailant in a face to face encounter, or is due to poisoning and disease caused by an impersonal corporation, the end result is similar.[17]

Are Street Crimes "Crimes"?

The large proportion of street crimes do not involve violence. They include theft, auto offences and "victimless crimes". "Victimless crimes" present a unique example of the politics of crime. The term "victimless crime" is applied to acts involving a willing exchange of goods and services and purported harms inflicted upon oneself. What is arguable is that victimization is more remote and/or difficult to ascertain than in "normal crimes". If someone steals a car from you or holds you up with a gun, you are obviously a victim and the other is the offender. However, public drunkenness, illicit use of drugs, gambling, abortion, prostitution, pornography and homosexuality usually

---

16 "Workers' Accident Rate Excessive," *The Calgary Herald*, June 10, 1976, p. 12.
17 "Threat of Mercury Poisoning Spreads Over Quebec," *The Calgary Herald*, April 2, 1976, p. 18 and Gail Singer and Bob Rodgers, "Mercury: The Hidden Poison in the Northern Rivers," *Saturday Night* (October, 1975), pp. 15-22.

involve a willing exchange of goods and services between two or more parties, but nonetheless are often criminalized in North America. For example, a prostitute exchanges sexual favours for money from the John. It is difficult to determine who is the victim and who is the criminal. While the John may believe that he has not had fair value for his money, it is unlikely he will become a complainant due to the illegal nature of the exchange. In the United States such crimes total nearly 50% of all crime,[18] while in Canada such acts constitute approximately 20% of the crime.[19] Therefore, since violent crimes account for less than 10% of all crime, "victimless crimes" are a larger proportion of the crime in North America.

These crimes are depicted in the media as inherently evil and subsequently dangerous. Stereotypes of the gambler, dope fiend, prostitute, homosexual and drunk present frightening pictures which evoke both pity and fear among the "morally superior".[20] While most users of illicit drugs, prostitutes, gamblers, homosexuals, and inebriates live relatively normal, law abiding lives apart from their appetites, crimes of violence, personal psychopathology, and sordid environments are dramatized in the mass media as typical of such "kinds of people" and their behaviour. Such representations fail to note that most of the limited violence and personal psychopathology which is evident is largely a product of restrictive laws, not of the behaviour *per se*. In fact, the consequences of making and maintaining such behaviours as criminal are likely more harmful than removing them from the auspices of the criminal law.

Report after report and study upon study have indicated that such "overcriminalization" produces the following negative consequences: artificially high profits and criminal monopolies; organized crime; secondary crime such as theft among addicts to support their habit; criminal subcultures; excessive expenditures of police and criminal justice resources; corruption of agents of the criminal justice system; contempt for the law and criminal justice system by offenders; infringement upon individual rights.[21]

---

18 Gilbert Geis, *Not the Law's Business?* (Washington, D.C.: U.S. Government Printing Office, 1972).

19 A principal reason for the smaller proportion of "victimless crimes" in Canada is the fact that drunkenness is no longer officially a crime in most provinces, homosexuality between consenting adults is no longer criminal, and prostitution per se is not criminal, although procuring, soliciting and operating a bawdy house are.

20 For example see Charles E. Reasons, "Images of Crime and the Criminal: The Dope Fiend Mythology", *Journal of Research In Crime and Delinquency*, 13 (July, 1976), pp. 133-44.

21 Norval Morris and Gordon Hawkins, *The Honest Politician's Guide to Crime*

Public policy criminalizing such behaviours is particularly subject to criticism within democratic societies.

To some extent crimes without victims are outlawed because of a benevolent interest in protecting an individual from himself. The difficulties here are acute. For one thing, in a democracy, freedom of an individual to determine what is best for himself, as long as he does not interfere with a similar freedom of others, is a prime ingredient. For another, it is dubious that the force of the criminal law upon marijuana smokers, abortion-seeking women, homosexuals and numbers players adds to the sum of their happiness and makes them better persons.[22]

Some students of crime are becoming increasingly aware of the ramifications of the trite observation that the formal cause of crime is the criminal law.

Our criminal law suffers from at least four defects. It fails to differentiate between real crimes and mere regulatory offenses. It descends into excessive detail. It uses a style and form of language that is inappropriate. And it is wedded to a Victorian philosophy which is now inadequate.[23]

The moral excesses in the criminal law can no longer be afforded. Overcriminalization in such areas as obscenity and pornography, unlawful gaming, and illicit drugs has produced more problems than it has solved. For example, there have been dramatic increases in the cost and effort of law enforcement, judicial and correctional personnel as they attempt to enforce narcotics legislation. The irrational and oppressive way we treat users of illicit drugs is hardly any better than the way witches were treated centuries ago. The "demonological" properties attributed to these drugs have little relation to their known effects, and our actions only appear to worsen the "drug problem" rather than decrease it.[24] Clearly the answer is not to increase penalties and personnel anticipating that there will be a decrease in illicit drug use with an increase in social control agents.

Control (Chicago: The University of Chicago Press, 1970); Commission on the Non-Medical Use of Drugs, *Final Report*, (Ottawa: Information Canada, 1973).

22 Gilbert Geis, "Crimes—But No Victims," *Reason*, 4 (September, 1972), pp. 16-18.

23 Law Reform Commission of Canada, *Our Criminal Law* (Ottawa: Information Canada, 1976), p. 35.

24 Edward Brecher, *Licit and Illicit Drugs* (Boston: Little, Brown and Company, 1972); Charles E. Reasons, "The Addict as a Criminal: Perpetuation of a Legend," *Crime and Delinquency*, 21 (January, 1975), pp. 19-27; Paul Grescoe, "A Case for Legal Heroine," *The Canadian, The Calgary Herald* (January 31, 1976), pp. 5-7.

Suite Crimes Have Victims

The difficulty in identifying victim(s) and offender(s) is a difference often noted between suite crime and violent street crime. While a visible, dramatic theft at gun point entails an obvious victim and a criminal, the taking of millions of dollars from millions of people through fraud or price fixing is less direct, with a more diffuse victim and offender.[25] For example, the theft of a worker's income tax, unemployment insurance and pension deductions by employers does not elicit the same response as bank robberies do, although it is a much more profitable type of crime. Failure to remit payroll deductions by employers in 1975 accounted for $7.9 million, while bank robbers, extortionists and kidnappers gained a profit of only $5.17 million in the same year.[26] A significant factor in such varying responses is the non-hostile, non-threatening nature of the setting and the fact that the offender is usually viewed as providing needed and legitimate goods and services.

That we are daily victimized is not usually recognized because, for example, we do not view the grocery store or department store as an accomplice, the manufacturer as a criminal, and ourselves as victims of rising costs.[27]

Even when "suite criminals" commit "common crimes" they tend to be evaluated differently. For example, if a person breaks into another's premises and takes something, the usual definition is breaking and entering or burglary, and the offender is subject to possible imprisonment. However, when the White House "Plumbers", CIA, FBI, RCMP or federal narcotics agents commit such behaviours, it is likely to be evaluated in terms of national defense and/or necessary in the war against crime and therefore immune from prosecution. The innumerable offenses of former U.S. President Nixon were viewed by many as the legitimate exercise of authority by the head of state.[28]

---

25 It should be noted that even in such "clear-cut" examples as homicide the victim may often bring about his own demise. The classic example of "victim-precipitated" homicide is the husband who verbally and/or physically abuses his spouse only to end up in the morgue due to gunshot or stabbing wounds. In other words, the "victim" was at one point the "offender". Such "mitigating factors" are legally admissible to reduce the offender's responsibility.

26 "Employer's Crimes Are Most Lucrative," *The Calgary Herald* (April 3, 1976), p. 4.

27 Charles E. Reasons, ed., *The Criminologist: Crime and the Criminal* (Pacific Palisades: Goodyear Publishing Co., 1974), p. 233.

28 William A. Dobrovir, Joseph P. Gebhardt, Samuel L. Buffone, and Andra N.

Furthermore, the public often identifies with the suite criminal who is a respectable businessman or civic official who contributes to the community and society. The Churchill Forest Industries scandal in Manitoba attests to the significance of appearance and status in suite crime. In a multi-million dollar swindle against the people of Manitoba, one Dr. Kosser and Associates put over one of the greatest cons in the annals of crime. In the end, it was estimated by an investigating commission that Dr. Kosser made about $26 million in excessive fees and paid no Canadian taxes on more than $33 million in earnings by setting up a network of companies. Left holding the bag were business and government leaders and, of course, the taxpayers of Manitoba.[29]

Why do we have such images of the crime problem? Where do we gain such perceptions? How are such images maintained? Our attitudes toward, and reactions to, crime are greatly affected by our perception of the nature of the crime problem. Our perception of the crime problem is largely related to our personal experiences and socialization. Since most of us do not experience rape, robbery or other crimes of violence, our perception of the nature and scope of "street crime", i.e., the crime problem, is largely a product of the diffusion of criminal conceptions and social types. Such images of crime and the criminal are provided us by our family, educational institutions, politicians and the mass media. Newspapers, television, radio, magazines, movies and official governmental reports continually provide us with definitions of the nature and scope of the crime problem. Such headlines as *Violent Crimes Up 10%, Rape Increases 100%, Murder Up 20%, Serious Crime on the Upsurge* convey to citizens that the crime problem (street crime) is increasing at an alarming rate. Uniform Crime Reports in both Canada and the United States emphasize "street crimes". Therefore, headlines such as *Corporate Crime Up 100%, Price Fixing Increases 50%, Corporate Crimes Death Toll Rises* are not usually found in the media.

Furthermore, the mass media is replete with crime drama depicting the crime problem and the actors involved in the "war against crime". For example, television provides almost daily doses of criminals, law enforcement officials, private investigators, judges, attorneys and correctional personnel. These grossly misrepresent the scope and nature of the crime problem and the criminal justice system.

The misinformation available through the mass media ... is overwhelming. Fiction about the crime and criminal justice is ridden with formula

Oakes, *The Offenses of Richard M. Nixon: A Guide to His Impeachable Crimes* (New York: Quadrangle/The New York Times Book Co., 1974).

29 "The C.F.I. Disaster," *The Calgary Herald* (October, 1974), p. 7.

and stereotype, its primary purpose being the satisfaction of the emotional needs of the viewing audience rather than the portrayal of crime in an authentic way. So also with crime news itself, which seldom portrays any but the most sensational and bizzare events.[30]

In spite of the above limitations, the mass media provide most citizens with their conceptions of the crime problem. Fear of "street crime" is widespread while fear of "suite crime" is minimal. The continual barrage of crime statistics we receive plays an important role in creating and maintaining a constant fear among the public. Both Canada and the United States have Uniform Crime Reports which are issued periodically during each year as the barometer on crime. While these reporting systems have been critically assailed for their problems,[31] they are taken by the public as valid and reliable indicators of crime. Therefore, increases in crime noted in the media may frighten the public even though there may be little basis for fear. For example, a survey team in Toronto found in 1970 that concern with crime for many citizens was partly an artificial creation and that people were more concerned about crime in the abstract rather than actually becoming a victim. It was concluded that crime, to some extent, is an imaginary problem which is manufactured in the minds of many people.[32] The definition of crime and the criminal is constantly reinforced through television dramas, newspaper headlines, police statistical reports, and political and civic speeches. The definitions of crime and the criminal provided in these sources do not accurately reflect the nature and scope of crime in Canada.

Why Study Suite Crime?

In contemporary Canadian society we are increasingly subject to ever larger government bureaucracies and corporations. In *The Vertical Mosaic*, John Porter reveals the extent of social stratification in Canada and the influence of elites upon our daily lives.[33] More recently, Wallace Clement in *The Canadian Corporate Elite* extensively docu-

---

30 Richard L. Henshel and Robert A. Silverman, "Perceptions and Criminal Process." *Canada Journal of Sociology,* 1 (Spring, 1975), p. 39. Also see, Richard L. Henshel and Robert A. Silverman, eds., *Perceptions In Criminology* (Toronto: Methuen, 1975).

31 For a summary of the major criticisms of these reporting systems see Edwin H. Sutherland and Donald Cressey, *Criminology,* 9th Edition (Philadelphia: J. B. Lippincott, 1974) and Robert A. Silverman and James Teevan, Jr., eds., *Crime In Canadian Society* (Toronto: Butterworth and Co. Ltd., 1975).

32 Michael E. Milakovitch and Kurt Weis, "Politics and Measures of Success In The War On Crime," *Crime and Delinquency,* 21 (January, 1975), pp. 1-10.

33 John Porter, *The Vertical Mosaic* (Toronto: University of Toronto Press, 1965).

ments the interlocking relationships between corporations and their influence upon Canadian society.[34] Whether corporations are multi-national or domestic, they are significant and influential in the operation of our society.[35] Canada subscribes to a liberal ideology emphasizing individualism, competition and equality of opportunity, yet it is clear that upward mobility is the exception rather than the rule, and that class lines are becoming more rigid.[36] One study of inequality points out that different class, status, ethnic and sex groups are not equally represented in terms of educational attainment, occupations or public office. It concludes by stating that: "However the inequalities arise, discrimination among class, status, ethnic, and sex groups is evidently a common feature of the Canadian political community."[37]

The structured inequalities in Canadian society are in part a product of corporate enterprise and economic concentration. Andrew Armitage identifies this process in *Canadian Social Welfare* by noting "the effect of the economic elites' influence on social welfare appears to lie principally in their power to restrict the extent of welfare transfer."[38] The great power wielded by corporations suggests they are immune from effective control. The dehumanization of our increasingly complex, urban society is compounded by the appearance, if not reality, of corporate impersonality and disregard for social justice. While citizens are told there are controls on corporations and their power and behaviour, few data exist concerning the nature of these controls and their effectiveness. Therefore, the analysis of suite crime is particularly significant as a means of making corporations publicly accountable for their behaviour. If the power and behaviour of corporations in Canada is not checked or goes unchallenged, citizens will certainly become skeptical with regard to their ability to influence public policy.

---

34 Wallace Clement, *The Canadian Corporate Elite* (Toronto: McClelland and Stewart Limited, 1975).

35 Robert Laxer, *Canada Ltd.* (Toronto: McClelland and Stewart, 1973).

36 Patricia Marchak, *Ideological Perspectives On Canada* (Toronto: McGraw-Hill Ryerson Limited, 1975); Sid Gilbert and Hugh A. McRoberts, "Differentiation and Stratification: The Issue of Inequality," in *Issues In Canadian Society*, eds. Dennis Forcese and Stephen Richer (Scarborough: Prentice-Hall of Canada, Ltd., 1975), pp. 91-136; Ian Adams et al. *The Real Poverty Report* (Edmonton: M. G. Hurtig Limited, 1971); David Smith and Lorne Tepperman, "Changes In The Canadian Business and Legal Elites, 1870-1970," *The Canadian Review of Sociology and Anthropology*, 11 (May, 1974), pp. 97-109.

37 Ronald Manzer, *Canada: A Socio-Political Report* (Toronto: McGraw-Hill Ryerson Limited, 1974).

38 Andrew Armitage, *Social Welfare In Canada* (Toronto: McClelland and Stewart, 1975), p. 75.

As previously discussed, suite crime costs the public more than street crime, while also entailing injuries and sometimes death. One author has pointed out the costs of monopolies in both the United States and Canada:

A U.S. study concludes that the overall cost of monopoly and shared monopoly in terms of lost production is somewhere between $48 billion and $60 billion annually. In Canada, lost output due to the same cause would be in the order of $4.5 to $6 billion dollars. The lost tax revenues alone from this wealth would go a long way towards ending poverty and pollution. The redistribution of income from monopoly profits that trans-fers income from consumers to shareholders is estimated at $2.3 billion annually in the U.S. and $2 to $3 billion in Canada. Monopolistic firms thus contribute to inequality, inflation and unemployment. Unemploy-ment results since monopolies, as noted, significantly reduce output which in turn reduces the number of workers who would otherwise be produc-ing.[39]

Thus, in terms of corporate accountability, financial cost, dehumaniza-tion and physical safety there is a need for studying suite crime.

We may have to reassess our understanding of crime and crimi-nality and its social sources. If the nature and scope of crime in a society reflects the nature of that society, then perhaps we get the criminals we deserve. Therefore, we need to direct our attention to possible criminogenic values in our society. Dominant values such as success, status and power seeking, monetary and material wealth, toughness, dupery and shrewdness contribute to both the "official criminal's" and "law-abiding citizen's" place in society.

While E. H. Sutherland noted long ago in *White Collar Crime* how similar the professional thief and corporate criminal were, we still have virtually no information on the scope and magnitude of corporate crime in Canada. There has been much study and public discussion of "street crime" and "street criminals", but we have yet to direct our attention to "suite crime" and "suite criminals". "Suite crime" may victimize more of the public for much more money than street crime. Furthermore, physical injury is more evident in suite crimes through accidents, diseases and deaths than is generally recognized. Such crimes may be more destructive to the members of society, economic-ally and physically, than all the "common crimes" and "common criminals" which we daily pursue through the criminal justice system. Such offenses tell us a great deal about ourselves and the criminogenic values in our society.

---

39 C. Gonick, *Inflation or Depression* (Toronto: James Lorimer Co., 1975), p. 22.

CHAPTER 2

Theories of Crime and Corporate Criminality

Business leaders are capable, emotionally balanced, and in no sense pathological . . . the assumption that an offender must have some such pathological distortion of the intellect or the emotions seems to one absurd, and if it is absurd regarding the crimes of businessmen, it is equally absurd regarding the crimes of persons in the lower economic class.

Edwin H. Sutherland, "The Crime of Corporations," in *Problems in Political Economy: An Urban Perspective*, ed., David M. Gordon (Lexington, Massachusetts: D. C. Heath, 1971), p. 310.

Kinds of People

Students of crime, like most of our citizens, have focused much of their time and effort on studying the criminal in order to find the causes of crime. This has led to many different explanations of criminal behaviour which look for the causes of criminal behaviour in the kinds of people who are identified as criminal. In the early part of the twentieth century such "kinds of people" theories[1] emphasized the assumed fact that there were born criminals. Generally it was believed that the born criminal was the cause of the crime problem and more particularly this problem was attributed to foreign races and nationalities.[2] The belief in the existence of innate differences between a criminal's behaviour and that of a non-criminal reflected an era of Social Darwinism, imperialism and racist ideology. In the United States, the president of the California State Law Enforcement League epitomized the public concern in a 1925 article which stated:

It is the law-breaking foreigners who we are talking about now. Schooled in low standards of morality, they seek to impose their European customs upon their new-found Land of Liberty. . . . Foreigners are predominant in all the big movements of lawlessness and these movements aim at anarchy.[3]

Similar ideas were prevalent in Canada as exemplified by the attitude towards the Chinese at the turn of the century: " . . . these Chinese are non-assimilative and having no intention of settled citizenship are in moral, social, sanitary status below the most inferior standard of Western life . . . "[4] Furthermore one student of the drug problem in early twentieth century Canada notes:

Previously attacked for their work habits, the Chinese were assailed as being selfish, slothful, weak, diseased, inefficient, untrustworthy and emasculated. In company with the racial assault against the Chinese,

---

1 For further elaboration upon these theories see Charles E. Reasons, "Social Thought and Social Structure: Competing Paradigms in Criminology," *Criminology,* 13 (November, 1975), pp. 332-65.

2 For elaboration upon the relationship between race and crime see Charles E. Reasons and Jack L. Kuykendall, eds., *Race, Crime and Justice* (Pacific Palisades: Goodyear Publishing Company, 1972); Marvin Wolfgang and Bernard Cohen, *Crime and Race: Conceptions and Misconceptions* (New York: Institute of Human Relations Press, 1970).

3 Edwin E. Grant, "Scum from the Melting Pot," *American Journal of Sociology,* 30 (May, 1925), pp. 641-51.

4 Report of the Commissioners Appointed to Inquire into the Subject of Chinese and Japanese Immigration into the Province of British Columbia, *Sessional Papers,* 54 (1902), p. 2.

vivid descriptions of the opium dens were invariably released to a horrified Canadian populace.[5]

The contemporary belief in the "born criminal" is found in the XYY chromosome anomaly. However, there does not appear to be much evidence to support the belief that those with an excessive male chromosome will be more violent. Nonetheless, it is an appealing hope within our traditional ideology of crime. It is comforting to most citizens to discover that criminals and other deviants are somehow fundamentally different from non-criminals and non-deviants. While this comforting myth has increasingly been disproven in recent years, the general public is very receptive to theories which continue to maintain such distinctions. Besides fulfilling the naïve hope for a simple, single source of criminality, " . . . it also provides a convenient moral advantage for both the community at large and those personally responsible for the offender's welfare, for all are relieved from blame for the behavioural consequences of what is a purely biological accident."[6]

Therefore, in spite of evidence to the contrary, many people want to believe in such an easy explanation and thus an apparently easy solution to the crime problem.[7]

The most widely accepted "kinds of people" theory today is the belief that those committing crime are psychologically different from

5 Terry L. Chapman, "The Drug Problem in Western Canada, 1900-1920" (unpublished Master's thesis, The University of Calgary, 1976), p. 143. For other elaborations of the racist "kinds of people" basis of the early "drug problem" in both Canada and the United States see Shirley J. Cook, "Canadian Narcotic Legislation, 1908-1923: A Conflict Model Interpretation," *The Canadian Review of Sociology and Anthropology*, 6 (1969), pp. 36-46; Charles E. Reasons, "The Politics of Drugs: An Inquiry into the Sociology of Social Problems," *The Sociological Quarterly*, 15 (Summer, 1974), pp. 391-412; and Gregory Yee Mark, "Racial, Economic and Political Factors in the Development of America's First Drug Laws," *Issues in Criminology*, 10 (Spring, 1975), pp. 49-73.

6 Richard G. Fox, "The XYY Offender: A Modern Myth," *The Journal of Criminal Law, Criminology and Police Science*, 62 (March, 1971), pp. 71-72. For other discussions of the XYY phenomenon see Brian C. Baker, "XYY Chromosome Syndrome and the Law," *Criminologica*, 7 (February, 1970), pp. 2-25; Theodore R. Sarbin and Jeffrey E. Miller, "Demonism Revisited: The XYY Chromosomal Anomaly," *Issues in Criminology*, 5 (Summer, 1970), pp. 195-207; Menachem Amir and Yitzchak Berman, "Chromosomal Deviation and Crime," *Federal Probation*, 34 (June, 1970), pp. 55-62; Barbara J. Cullition, "Patient's Rights: Harvard is Site of Battle over X and Y Chromosomes," *Science*, 186 (November, 1974), pp. 715-17.

7 A professor in the Department of Genetics at The University of Alberta proposed the following "solution" to this problem in *Science*, 164 (1969), p. 1117: "All boys and men who are under lawful restraint should be classified into XY and XYY categories so that the best treatment can be ascertained and carried out. . . . The probability factor makes the criminal XYY a predictably dangerous person and the standards of the duty to take care should accordingly be raised."

those not committing crime.[8] A great deal of research and many programs of rehabilitation are based upon this assumption. In fact, it would be correct to say that our contemporary programs of rehabilitation are founded upon the notion that the offender is somehow psychologically "sick". Therefore a medical model is utilized, in which the criminal (patient) is diagnosed through tests and interviews. Based upon this diagnosis a prognosis is given which indicates the possibility of "curing" the criminal, after which he is treated for his problems. Therefore, like a diseased patient, the criminal is diagnosed, prognosed, prescribed and treated for his "illness". Although such a theory is quite compatible with our emphasis upon individualism and personal culpability, it presents somewhat of a dilemma for the offender. While the offender is legally responsible for his actions, he is treated for the malady which determined his behaviour through psychiatric, psychological casework, probation and parole practices. More importantly, we do not have any good evidence supporting the assumption that criminals differ significantly from non-criminals psychologically. One criminology student describes the criminal from this viewpoint:

The medical model has prompted a long and futile search for the psychological counterparts of germs and tumors. Unfortunately there are no infected organs or disease entities that can be identified as the causes of deviant behaviour. Instead we infer deviant personality types and emotional disorders from our observations of behaviour. Then we use our psychological constructs to explain the very phenomena from which they were inferred in the first place. In short, deviance, including delinquency, is fundamentally different from physical illness. It has no existence apart from the judgements people make about particular kinds of behaviour.[9]

In spite of the lack of supporting data for the psychological abnormality theory, it still receives a great deal of professional and public support. For example, dangerous offender legislation is in the Criminal Code, despite the fact that we have no valid and reliable means for predicting dangerous offenders. In an extensive review of scientific

---

8 For example see Gordon W. Russon, "Interpersonal Adequacy: A Behavioural Determinant," *Canadian Journal of Criminology and Corrections*, 16 (July, 1974), pp. 393-402; G. Barry Morris, "The Criminal in Relation to the Self-Actualization and Rational-Emotive Theories," *Crime et/and Justice*, 4 (1976), pp. 40-43; G. Barry Morris, "Irrational Beliefs of Prison Inmates," *Canadian Journal of Criminology and Corrections*, 18 (July, 1976), pp. 181-89; Lorraine Wilgosh and Daniel Paitich, "Characteristics of Juvenile Offenders, Grouped According to Psychiatric Description and Their Parents," *Canadian Journal of Criminology and Corrections*, 18 (July, 1976), pp. 267-71.

9 Robert W. Balch, "The Medical Model of Delinquency," *Crime and Delinquency*, 21 (April, 1975), p. 118.

literature about predicting dangerousness, a criminologist concludes that:

It should be clear by now that given the present state of knowledge and expertise respecting the prediction of future dangerousness, there are inherent dangers in enacting dangerous offender legislation. While there may well be merit in repealing the present habitual offender and dangerous sex offender legislation, this does not necessitate replacing that legislation with legislation which may well be as bad (if not worse) as that which is repealed.[10]

If the assumption of psychological abnormality is generally incorrect for "common criminals" who commit street crimes, it would also appear to be invalid for suite criminals. As the noted student of corporate crime, E. H. Sutherland, stated: "We have no reason to think that General Motors has an inferiority complex or that the Aluminum Company of America has a frustration-aggression complex, or that U.S. Steel has an Oedipus complex, or that Armour Company has a death wish or that the Duponts desire to return to the womb."[11]

Kinds of Environment

Within the last few decades there has emerged a major competing theory about the causes of criminal behaviour which locates the problem in the criminal's environment. In this approach various "kinds of environment" are emphasized in explaining why people commit crime. More specifically, emphasis is placed upon the family, peer group and conditions in the community such as poor housing, unemployment, inadequate educational facilities, discrimination against ethnic groups, etc. Therefore, the criminal is viewed as a "normal" product of abnormal and pathological conditions. In a recent book authored by the former Executive Director of the John Howard Society of Ontario, A. M. Kirkpatrick, and the Executive Director of the Canadian Criminology and Corrections Association, W. T. McGrath, such an approach is emphasized when discussing "the roots of crime": "The corrosive effects of substandard or slum areas in our cities should be understood, since they are areas of infection which may corrupt all our

---

10 John F. Klein, "The Dangerousness of Dangerous Offender Legislation: Forensic Folklore Revisited," *Canadian Journal of Criminology and Corrections*, 18 (April, 1976), p. 118.

11 E. H. Sutherland, "Crime and Business," *The Annals*, 217 (1941), p. 96. While this reifies corporations as persons with personalities, the same argument is applicable to individuals culpable for suite crime. For example see Gilbert Geis, ed., *White Collar Criminal* (New York: Atherton Press, 1968).

children and youth."[12] Rather than being a product of internal psychological predispositions, criminal behaviour is viewed as a response to one's environment. Studies are done comparing offenders and non-offenders in terms of employment, income, location of residence, family stability, education, ethnicity, among other characteristics. The difference between the criminal and the non-criminal is found in the external circumstances of the offender. For example, official data on serious offenders in Canada tell us that they are disproportionately from the lower class,[13] and particularly native people.[14] It would seem that the condition of poverty is closely related to crime. The implications of this finding might lead us to attempt to eliminate poverty by changing the economic system or by better equipping the poor to battle impoverishment. Since the dominant ideology in Canada emphasizes individualism and self-help, our efforts to change the nature of inequality in Canada are largely directed to changing the poor.[15] Therefore, manpower training programs are a major facet of the attack on poverty. In the area of rehabilitation of criminals, much attention is given to providing some type of job training and/or experience for the offender. Seldom are attempts made to change the nature of the economic system in order to lessen inequalities as a preventive measure in the fight against crime. The Law Reform Commission addresses this issue by noting that laws on property offences should be simplified and reassessed with regard to the role of property in our society. "Some property offences are a product of the unjust distribution of property in our society and such 'crimes' call not for criminal law and punishment, but rather for some genuine social reform."[16] This observation has quite radical implications for social change in our society, but most "kinds of environment" theories focus upon changing the offender to fit within the current conditions of society. For example, while much has been said and written about the relationship between poverty and crime, most rehabilitation programs based upon "kinds of environment" theories emphasize preparation/change of the individual to fit into the current economic system rather

---

12 A. M. Kirkpatrick and W. T. McGrath, *Crime and You* (Toronto: Macmillan of Canada, 1976), pp. 156-57. For an attempt to combine environmental design with crime control see C. R. Jeffery, *Crime Prevention through Environmental Design* (Beverly Hills, California: Sage Publications, 1971).

13 Gwynn Netler, *Explaining Crime* (New York: McGraw Hill, 1974).

14 James Frideres, *Canada's Indians: Contemporary Conflicts* (Scarborough: Prentice-Hall of Canada, Ltd., 1974).

15 For a discussion of the ideological basis for our approach see M. Patricia Marchak, *Ideological Perspectives on Canada* (Toronto: McGraw-Hill Ryerson Limited, 1975).

16 Law Reform Commission of Canada, *Our Criminal Law* (Ottawa: Information Canada, 1976), p. 15.

than changing the nature of jobs and work obligations to fit the needs of individual citizens.

Both the "kinds of people" theories and the "kinds of environment" theories of criminal behaviour compare criminals and non-criminals in order to discover the correlates and ultimately the causes of crime. However, such comparisons have largely failed:

In the two approaches presented so far, the focus is on the criminal. He is seen as being sick or reacting criminally to unmet needs and deprivations. This badness, sickness or delinquent responsiveness to unmet needs sets these people apart from the population at large. The criminal population is expected to reveal significant differences when compared with the non-delinquent population in a number of psychological, sociological, demographic and other characteristics. Many researches were conducted along these lines. The various summaries of these researches fail however to indicate these dissimilarities.[17]

While poverty, broken homes and ethnic minority status are noted in most texts as significant causes of crime, what can be said about the corporate executives who violate the law? They do not live in poverty, and in most cases have stable homes and family lives and are members of the majority ethnic group. This suggests that the previously noted relationship between crime and certain "kinds of environments" is only applicable to certain types of offences. Again we must become aware of the multitude of behaviours defined as criminal and realize that most of society's attention is given to "street crime" and thus "street criminals". Therefore, relationships between social class, ethnicity, family life and crime are due to a selective definition of crime. That is, the attention of law enforcement and the general public is focused upon "street crimes" such as robbery, auto theft and murder which do take place more frequently among certain classes and ethnic groups; however, such economic offences as fraud, price-fixing, income tax evasion and such violent offences as lack of safety standard maintenance, systematically defective products, poisoning of the air, water or food gain little public or law-enforcement attention.

The Law Reform Commission observes that in theory the principle of justice dictates that equality of treatment be given throughout the criminal justice system without regard to social class, ethnicity, or other "irrelevant traits". However:

In practice, the penalty often depends, not on the nature of the crime, but on the person who commits it. Our prison population, for example,

17 Yona Cohn, "Vacancies for Criminals," *Criminology Made in Canada,* 3 (1975), p. 194.

contains a quite unrepresentative proportion of poor, of disadvantaged and of native offenders. The richer you are, the better your chance of getting away with something. <u>Is it that rich men make the laws and so what rich men do is not a crime but simply shrewd business practice? Or is it that position and wealth protect the rich against intervention?... For all the respect we pay to justice and equality, we still have one law for the rich and another for the poor</u> [emphasis added].[18]

In the above statement, the Law Reform Commission of Canada addresses two increasingly significant issues in contemporary criminology: (1) do laws reflect some interests more than others? and (2) does the criminal justice system discriminate against some groups compared to other groups? Both of these issues are significant for students of law. While traditional criminology focused largely upon characteristics of the offender (kinds of people and kinds of environment), some criminologists are advocating that we study the way in which laws arise and how they operate. We are reminded again of a long-standing truism for students of the law: *"The formal cause of crime is the criminal law."* Until recently, criminologists have neglected this observation.

Therefore, one might study offenders all his life without questioning how the specific behavioural acts became criminalized or the subsequent processing of such actors in the criminal justice system. In fact, this has been a major oversight of criminologists. While going to great ends to scrutinize, characterize, count, and describe the criminal, little effort has been given to the other areas of criminological import.[19]

While criminology has been defined as the study of the sociology of law, causes of criminal behaviour and penology,[20] relatively little attention has been given to the sociology of law.

The relative neglect of sociological analysis of the law is related to a number of factors. The lack of legal studies as part of a liberal arts education has hampered such inquiry. There is a mystique and sacredness attached to the law and legal bodies which is in part due to the general public's lack of knowledge concerning the law. This was not always the case, however: Blackstone's Commentaries were lectures given at Oxford University to liberal arts students; American colonists acquired legal education in order to establish control systems in their

18 Law Reform Commission, *Our Criminal Law*, p. 12.
19 Charles E. Reasons, "Social Thought and Social Structure: The Criminologist, Crime and the Criminal," in *The Criminologist: Crime and the Criminal*, ed., Charles E. Reasons (Pacific Palisades: Goodyear Publishing Company, 1974), p. 6.
20 Edward H. Sutherland and Donald R. Cressey, *Criminology* (Philadelphia: J. B. Lippincott Company, 1972), p. 3.

new land. Edmund Burke's comments on the influence of Blackstone reflect this interest:

In no country perhaps in this world is the law so general a study. The profession itself is numerous and powerful, and in most provinces it takes the lead. The greater number of deputies sent to the congress were lawyers. . . . I have been told by an eminent bookseller, that in no branch of his business, after tracts of popular devotion, were so many books as those on the law exported to the plantations.[21]

The basic fact is that law and legal education are a source of power and have been principally in the hands of those making policy. With the professionalization of law and its institutionalization in the form of law schools, a professional monopoly was established concerning the diffusion of legal education.

Another major impediment to the sociological study of the law has been the barrier of discipline and training. Both sociologists and lawyers have created a professional jargon and way of looking at things which have largely inhibited joint efforts. Furthermore, the empirical thrust of North American sociology kept many from investigating law and its "speculative" nature, rather than following European scholars in their socio/legal analysis.

Finally, although criminologists have long been concerned with the control of human behaviour, questioning normative practices, that is, laws, was not of major importance. The laws were a given and the focus of attention was upon those who violated the law.

Power/Conflict

Some students of crime have more recently viewed social conflict and differences in power as significant factors in explaining crime in a society. As one criminologist observes, new questions must be asked: "Among those questions are, for example, the following: 'what may we properly demand of a system of criminal justice?', 'what are the political aspects and consequences of the use of criminalization to ensure social control?', and 'what is the social cost of the use of that process?'."[22]

These criminologists have explicitly recognized the importance of power, politics and people in creating, sustaining and shaping condi-

---

21 Quoted in Harold J. Berman and William R. Greiner, *The Nature and Functions of Law* (Brooklyn: The Foundation Press, 1966), p. 1.

22 Yvon Dandurand, "The Professional Criminologist in Canada," *Criminology Made in Canada*, 3 (1976), p. 159.

tions conducive to criminality which are identified by kinds of environment theories. For example, the finding that poverty can be associated with certain kinds of criminality and victimization might provoke the analyst to ask why such large inequities in the distribution of wealth and goods exist in a "society of plenty". This might lead to a critical analysis of economic policy rather than of criminal characteristics.

Whose Law? What Order?

Increasing awareness regarding the political nature of crime and the law has arisen with heightened conflict between traditionally powerless groups, e.g., students and youth, poor and non-white, and those in power. Traditionally submerged in a consensus perspective of society which views the state as neutral, the criminologist has been recently struck by the increasing number of questions about the legitimacy of specific laws and ultimately the authority of the state. Some criminologists have begun to investigate critically the origin, enforcement and administration of laws within the context of interests, power and conflict.

To understand the law, its enforcement and administration, power/conflict writers call for a demystification of the conceptions of the nature and function of law and place it in the context of power, politics and people. Chambliss and Seidman[23] suggest that the presentation of a "mythical" consensus perspective of the law is a normal occurrence in law schools, political science courses on law, criminology, and high school courses dealing with the law.

A number of schools of jurisprudence including natural, cultural and historical, have denied that law-makers have value choices in the creation of laws.[24] These schools of legal philosophy suggest that the law and its agents (including enforcers and administrators) stand above and apart from society, comprising a neutral body within which social struggle and conflict take place. This consensus perspective views the state as a value-neutral organ for the resolution of conflict. Therefore, although the adversary proceedings put the state against the accused, it occurs within the "neutral" framework of the court. The judge epitomizes the even-handed, non-biased, neutral arbitrator of institutionalized conflict. This perspective is held by most citizens and such beliefs are central to our democratic ideals of the "blind" nature

---

23 William Chambliss and Robert Seidman, *Law, Order and Power* (Reading, Massachusetts: Addison-Wesley, 1971).
24 Edwin Schur, *Law and Society* (New York: Random House, 1969).

of justice and the equity of our political and legal system. The presumed non-political and unbiased nature of the judicial system has obscured the basically political nature of crime and the law.

Other schools of jurisprudence suggest that law is a legitimizing weapon of the highest order, and those making, enforcing and administering laws are merely attempting to perpetrate the existing state and its social order.[25] These schools have demystified the nature of laws by emphasizing that they are man-made and state-given, not found in some natural state of things beyond the influence and control of man. Rather than the state and its legal actors being value-free, these perspectives invest participants in the legal system with values, feelings and bias which influence their actions. Rather than being a neutral framework for the collective interests of society, law is an instrument used by those in power to maintain their position and privilege. As one University of Toronto criminologist argues, the power/conflict conception of law is superior to the neutral approach. "A superior alternative is the conception of law as power, i.e., a set of resources whose control and mobilization can in many ways...generate and exacerbate conflicts rather than resolving or softening them."[26]

Therefore, viewing the law as an instrument of interests has become a growing area of concern among some criminologists. Quinney's text, *The Social Reality of Crime*, articulates what many dissident leaders of the 1960s suggested, that criminal law is largely made, enforced and administered by interest groups for their own gains. That text stands in stark contrast to traditional criminology texts in theory and presentation. The theory of the social reality of crime consists of six propositions that emphasize the political nature of crime as a phenomenon created in a heterogeneous society characterized by conflict. Quinney has presented one of the best statements of the power/conflict paradigm as a viable alternative to traditional paradigms.[27] This "power/conflict" perspective demystifies the traditional conception of criminal and non-criminal which prevades criminology. By focusing upon the political nature of criminal definitions, their appli-

25 Chambliss and Seidman, *Law, Order and Power.*

26 Austin T. Turk, "Law as a Weapon in Social Conflict," *Social Problems,* 23 (February, 1976), p. 276.

27 See Richard Quinney, *The Social Reality of Crime* (Boston: Little, Brown, 1970). For other elaborations of the power/conflict perspective see Robert S. Denisoff and Charles H. McCaghy, eds., *Deviance, Conflict and Criminality* (Chicago: Rand McNally, 1973); Charles McCaghy, *Deviant Behaviour: Crime, Conflict and Interest Groups* (New York: Macmillan Publishing Co. Inc., 1976); Ian Taylor, Paul Walton and Jock Young, *The New Criminology: For a Social Theory of Deviance* (London: Routledge and Kegan Paul, 1973); Austin T. Turk, *Criminality and Legal Order* (Chicago: Rand McNally, 1969).

cation and enforcement, the "power/conflict" perspective asserts that crime is a product of current power differentials and conflicting world views. Crime is a definition of behaviour made by officials of the state and not inherent in an act. Those behaviours which are offensive to the powers that be will be made crimes. Rather than focusing upon the "common crimes" of the "common criminals", emphasis is placed upon the lawless behaviour of the state and those in positions of power. The Watergate Affair, Harbour Gate, Lockheed deal, ITT, Sky Shops, increasing pervasive repression of political dissidents, government lawlessness, corporate and white collar crime, and the violence of continual hunger, impoverishment, poor housing, sexism and racial oppression are identified as "the crime problem". When attending to "common crimes" and "common criminals", emphasis is placed upon the oppressive, arbitrary and self-serving nature of the criminal justice system and its injustices from the criminal's perspective.

Order and Conflict Analysis

The "kinds of people" and "kinds of environment" theories of crime tend to support the status quo and focus upon the characteristics of the criminal. These "order" approaches have been prevalent in the study of crime for some time.[28] Within recent years some students of crime have given attention to how laws are made and to their administration. This emphasis has produced a focus on power and conflict as essential aspects for understanding crime and criminality. A major proponent of the conflict perspective has presented a diagrammatic comparison of the explanations of the order and conflict theories about the causes and consequences of both criminal behaviour and criminal law.[29]

Table 2-1 provides a contrast of order and conflict theories of crime. The order perspective views criminal law as reflecting the common good and controlling the criminal, while the conflict perspective sees ruling class interests as causing criminal law to be enacted in order to maintain class dominance. Criminal behaviour is due to inadequate socialization and it establishes moral boundaries according to order theorists, while a conflict perspective presents class divisions as the cause of criminal behaviour and the reduction of class strains as its consequence.

---

28 John Horton, "Order and Conflict Theories of Social Problems," *American Journal of Sociology* (May, 1966), pp. 701-13.

29 William Chambliss, *Functional and Conflict Theories of Crime*, MSS Modular Publications, 17 (New York, 1974).

TABLE 2-1.   ORDER AND CONFLICT THEORIES OF CRIME*

	Criminal Law		Criminal Behaviour	
	Cause	Consequence	Cause	Consequence
Conflict Paradigm	Ruling class interests	Provide state coercive force to repress the class struggle and to legitimize the use of this force	Class divisions which lead to class struggle	Crime serves the interests of the ruling class by reducing strains inherent in the capitalist mode of production
Order Paradigm	Customary beliefs that are codified in state law	To establish procedures for controlling those who do not comply with customs	Inadequate socialization	To establish the moral boundaries of the community

*Adapted from William J. Chambliss, *Functional and Conflict Theories of Crime* ((New York: MSS Modular Publications, Inc.) 1974.

One economist has suggested that lower class, organized and corporate crime can be explained as rational reactions to the respective circumstances of the criminals involved.[30] Due to the oppressive circumstances of low income life, crime represents a rational response to economic options. Organized crime in areas of great public demand (drugs, gambling, prostitution) are perfectly rational responses to economic demands. Finally, corporate crime is an eminently rational way to earn profits in capitalist societies, with high profits and little chance of detection and prosecution, much less conviction. Therefore, given their differences in power and subsequent economic alternatives, each form of criminal activity is a rational way to survive. This is quite contrary to the order perspective assumption that criminals are largely pathological and irrational in their behaviour. While these differences in approach are presented in "ideal type" form, they nonetheless provide a means of noting the differences in order and conflict theories of crime. These varying evaluations of the causes and consequences of criminal law and criminal behaviour provide a basis for reaction to crime.

30 David M. Gordon, "Capitalism, Class and Crime in America," *Crime and Delinquency*, 19 (April, 1973), pp. 163-86.

In order to understand contemporary reactions to certain behaviours defined as criminal, we should look historically at the emergence of crime as a product of the nation state. Criminal law is characterized by its public nature, state origin and politically unifying role. To say that criminal law is inherently political is at once a trite truism and a blasphemous assertion. Such a statement is manifestly true if the criminal law purportedly reflects the desires and goals of a political unit (the nation state), while it may appear to be a blasphemous assertion for those who divorce the law from politics. To provide a clearer picture of the political nature of the criminal law one need only view the nation state and subsequent criminal law as a relatively "new" creation in man's history. How were "bad" behaviours dealt with prior to the emergence of the nation state?

From Tribal to State Law

Between 400 AD and 1200 AD the foundation of contemporary criminal law developed in England.[31] Tribal law was replaced during this period by a common law system which is now the basis of our contemporary legal system. How did tribal law differ from state law? Table 2-2 briefly outlines the changes in the two systems of dispute settlement.

TABLE 2-2. CHANGES FROM TRIBAL TO STATE LAW

Legal Factor	Tribal Law	State Law
Unit of justice	Family	State
Jurisdictional ties	Blood	Territory
Basis of responsibility	Collective	Individual
Method of dispute settlement	Feud or compensation	Punishment

31 Much of the following discussion is based upon Clarence R. Jeffery, "The Development of Crime in Early English Society," *Journal of Criminal and Law, Criminology and Police Science*, 47 (March-April, 1957), pp. 647-66; Mark C. Kennedy, "Beyond Incrimination," *Catalyst*, 6 (Summer, 1970), pp. 1-37. While the tribes discussed above were evident in Western Europe, native North Americans (Indians) had similar legal systems based upon the same ingredients. In colonizing native North Americans, Europeans imposed their Anglo-Saxon legal system upon indigenous people. While a few reservations still handle lesser offences through a tribal system of justice in the U.S., it is largely a carbon copy of the Anglo-Saxon system rather than the traditional tribal system. Another remnant of tribal justice in North America was that existing in the Southern United States' backward areas. The Hatfield-McCoy stories of feuds were based upon a quasi-tribal system of justice which survived into the twentieth century.

Under the tribal system the family, defined on the basis of blood ties, was the basic unit determining and administering justice. With the demise of the tribal system the nation state which was defined on the basis of territorial ties, emerged as the basic unit to determine and administer justice. For example, under tribal law if one member of a tribe took the life of a person from another tribe, the offender's tribe would be collectively held responsible, not the individual killer. Subsequently, the victim's tribe might attempt to settle the debt by taking the life of *any* member of the other tribe. This action might precipitate a feud which could go on for some time. Another possible method of resolving the harm would be by extracting compensation from the offending tribe. Such compensation might be in the form of valued goods paid for the deceased. Within the context of the nation state, the killer would be held individually responsible for the act and would be punished by agents of the state through execution. The nation state does not allow compensation even if the family of the deceased agreed to a settlement. Such behaviour is viewed as a crime against the nation state, not just an individual.

What occurred between 400 AD and 1200 AD to bring about such a change in legal systems? Political unification of tribal settlements—largely due to civil wars among local military bands, the Danish invasion of the tenth century, and the acceptance of Christianity as the religion—greatly aided the rise of the nation state. When William became King of England in 1066 the Norman nobles replaced the Saxons as the upper class and a system of common law emerged as law common to all people of England. Subsequently, the state took the place of kinsmen and no longer allowed private settlements of a criminal case.

English criminal law came about to protect particular interests primarily those of the King. The criminal law placed the affairs of his subjects under his jurisdiction. The powerful landholders and the church could no longer freely create and administer law in their own courts. Law that affected the nation was now the King's law, the nation's interests were those of the King.[32]

These changes in legal systems are related to changes in the nature of societies. In the stateless society more emphasis was placed upon compromise or the "give a little, get a little" theory of dispute settlement.[33]

Such a means of resolving disputes usually occurs where a contin-

---

32 Richard Quinney, *Criminology* (Boston: Little, Brown, 1975), p. 47.

33 See Chambliss and Seidman, *Law, Order and Power*, pp. 28-36.

ued relationship between disputants is anticipated. In other words, in a small, homogeneous society where continued, close relationships are anticipated, compromise and negotiation are important. In complex, heterogeneous, stratified societies the dispute settling process determines that one party is right and one is wrong, i.e., winner take all or a zero sum game. Thus, in contemporary North America, the law and legal system are largely based on determining victims and criminals, right or wrong, transgressed and transgressor based upon the "winner take all" philosophy. The development of this approach to conflict resolution is very much related to the extent of stratification in a nation state. "The more economically stratified a society becomes, the more it becomes necessary for the dominant groups in the society to enforce through coercion the norms of conduct which guarantee their supremacy."[34]

Therefore, in our highly complex and stratified society one should expect that those in the lower classes would be disproportionately represented in statistics on crime and the criminal justice system. Furthermore, as the diversity and complexity of society increases there is an increase in the number of formal agents of social control. The interests of the dominant and powerful segments of the nation state will be those incorporated into and protected by the law and legal system.

State Interests and the Study of Crime

A classic example of the significance of dominant group interests in defining crime is the emergence of the law of theft.[35] Prior to the fifteenth century there was no legal conception of theft in the criminal law as we know it today. However, in the Carrier's Case of 1473 the legal concept of theft was established and has subsequently flourished in contemporary western laws. In the Carrier's Case, a transporter of goods took the goods he was entrusted with, converted them to his own use, and was subsequently charged with a felony. Prior to this case, if one took goods entrusted to him it was not theft. The burden was upon those entrusting goods to others to find someone who was reliable and trustworthy. If you failed to get someone who could be

---

34 *Ibid.*, pp. 33-34. While social psychological coercion through the family, educational institutions and other forms of socialization is least costly in terms of manifest conflict, ultimately the use of physical coercion is evident through legal sanctions.

35 See Jerome Hall, *Theft, Law and Society*, 2nd edition (Indianapolis: Bobbs-Merrill, 1952).

trusted you might lose quite a lot of your goods. Thus, possession was ten-tenths of the law. However, in this case the King's judges ruled the transporter guilty of theft, contrary to all legal precedent. Why the dramatic change?

In fifteenth-century Europe the commercial revolution was taking place and the old feudal structure based upon agriculture was giving way to a new order based upon industry and trade. More significantly, the King was very much involved in commercial activities, including trade, and could not allow such wrongdoings. Since the courts were subservient to the wishes of King Edward IV, the decision against the merchant should have been anticipated. Notwithstanding prior common law, the state's (King's) interests were best served by expanding the definition of theft under criminal law to better protect the commercial interests of the state and the new entrepreneurial class.

The above example of theft points out the significance of the state in the study of crime. An understanding of the dynamics of the state is crucial for the study of crime in contemporary society. The concept of the state stands for various specific institutions which are connected to one another and thus comprise the state.[36] The state system includes the following elements: the government; the administration; the military and the police; the judiciary; and units of subcentral government.[37] In capitalist nations such as Canada, the dominant economic class largely controls the state.[38] As one student of the state notes: "What the evidence conclusively suggests is that in terms of social origin, education, and class situation, the men who have manned all command positions in the state system have largely, and in many cases overwhelmingly, been drawn from the world of business and property, or from the professional middle class."[39]

The significance of discussing the role of the state in the study of crime is the realization that state interests represent dominant interests, and in terms of capitalist society, this means economic elites. In discussing crime control in capitalist society one criminologist notes the significance of the state:

The state is . . . a political organization created out of force and coercion.

---

36 Ralph Milibrand, *The State in Capitalist Society* (London: The Camelot Press Ltd., 1969), pp. 49-67.

37 *Ibid.*, p. 66.

38 Khayyon Zev Paltriel, *Political Party Financing in Canada* (Toronto: McGraw-Hill, 1970); John Porter, *The Vertical Mosaic* (Toronto: University of Toronto Press, 1965); Wallace Clement, *The Canadian Corporate Elite* (Toronto: McClelland and Stewart, 1975); Peter Newman, *The Canadian Establishment* (Toronto: McClelland and Stewart, 1975).

39 Newman, *The Canadian Establishment*, p. 388.

The state is established by those who desire to protect their material basis and who have the power (because of material means) to maintain the state. The law in capitalist society gives political recognition to powerful private interests.[40]

Thus, within the context of the conflict paradigm presented earlier in Table 2-1, the criminal law reflects the concerns and interests of dominant class interests. Since in our capitalist society it is mainly economic and business elites which control the state, it follows that the legal system will principally reflect their values and concerns.

State Interests and Anti-Combines Legislation

While there is an increasing body of evidence supporting the conflict interpretation of the creation of laws, much of this literature deals with "victimless crimes" and concerns the United States.[41] The only analysis in Canada investigating these perspectives presents a conflict interpretation of Canadian drug legislation.[42]

Combines legislation provides an apparent contradiction to the conflict perspective assumption that laws are specifically aimed at maintaining dominant class interests. Chambliss discusses this flaw in conflict analysis by noting that conflict analysis has not generally

40 Richard Quinney, *Critique of the Legal Order: Crime Control in Capitalist Society* (Boston: Little, Brown and Company, 1974), p. 52. Undoubtedly some will suggest we are neglecting the elite interests reflected in purportedly non-capitalist societies such as Yugoslavia, Cuba, People's Republic of China, and the Soviet Union. However, our concern is with the capitalist state of Canada. We would agree with Chambliss and Seidman, *Law*, p. 4, that a state's legal order is a self-serving system to maintain power and privilege and that *this is inevitable*.

41 William Chambliss, "A Sociological Analysis of the Law of Vagrancy," *Social Problems*, 12 (Summer, 1964), pp. 67-77; Joseph Gusfield, *Symbolic Crusade* (Bloomington: University of Illinois Press, 1963); Otto Kirchheimer, *Political Justice: The Use of the Legal Procedure for Political Ends* (Princeton: Princeton University Press, 1961); Charles E. Reasons, "The Politics of Drugs: An Inquiry in the Sociology of Social Problems," *Sociological Quarterly*, 15 (Summer, 1974), pp. 381-404; Pamela Roby, "Politics and Criminal Law: Revision of the New York State Penal Law on Prostitution," *Social Problems*, 17 (Summer, 1969), pp. 83-109; Edwin Schur, *Crimes Without Victims* (Englewood Cliffs: Prentice-Hall, 1965); Ingeborg Paulus, "Law-making: From Bill to Act, a Status Passage," *The Canadian Review of Sociology and Anthropology*, 12 (November, 1975), pp. 500-13; Otto Newman, "The Ideology of Social Problems: Gambling, A Case Study," *The Canadian Review of Sociology and Anthropology*, 12 (November, 1975), pp. 541-50.

42 Shirley Cook, "Canadian Narcotics Legislation, 1908-1923; A Conflict Model Interpretation," *The Canadian Review of Sociology and Anthropology*, 6 (February, 1969), pp. 36-46. More recently McDonald has presented an excellent overview of consensus and conflict perspectives with both cross-cultural and Canadian analysis. See Lynn McDonald, *The Sociology of Law and Order* (Montreal: Book Center, 1976), especially Chapter 7: "Law and Order in Canada," pp. 221-254.

realized the extent to which laws will be passed in order to reduce the manifestation of conflict between social classes.

An historical analysis of such laws would show that they emerge during times of open conflict between social classes and that the real extent to which the laws interfere with capitalists' interests through enforcement, subsequent legislation, and court decisions is negligible [emphasis added].[43]

Furthermore, Chambliss suggests that traditional conflict analysis has failed to study the administration of laws and the extent to which this reflects elite interests. Finally, conflict theorists have tended to neglect the fact that there may on occasion be interelite conflict which is reflected in legislation.

The following analysis will provide an assessment of the usefulness of a conflict interpretation of the emergence and change of anti-combines legislation in Canada. While such analysis has been undertaken in the United States, comparable studies are lacking in Canada. We will assess both the original anti-combines legislation and subsequent changes within the context of the conflict approach. By looking not only at the original legislation but also later revisions, the nature and extent of interest groups and their varying impact will be evident.[44] Within the conflict perspective, the origin, enforcement and administration of combines laws become the major areas of analysis, viewing the law as an instrument of the powerful rather than as the servant of the "public" interest.[45] The role of the state in serving elite interests is a major part of our inquiry.

While anti-combines legislation entails only certain types of corporate crime, it reflects dominant values which are the basis for other legislation. The federal government of Canada contends that it is an "independent institution, representing everyone equally and not the interests of one sector over others."[46] It was the federal government that introduced anti-combines legislation, the express purpose of which

---

43 Chambliss, *Functional and Conflict Theories of Crime*, p. 22.

44 For a recent discussion of interest groups and legislation see Andrew Hopkins, "On the Sociology of Criminal Law," *Social Problems*, 22 (June, 1975), pp. 608-19.

45 For a presentation of some of the few studies in Canada focusing upon interests in the making of laws and their administration see Craig T. O. Boydell, Paul C. Whitehead and Carl F. Grindstaff, eds., *The Administration of Criminal Justice in Canada* (Toronto: Holt, Rinehart, and Winston of Canada, 1974); A. Paul Pross, ed., *Pressure Group Behaviour in Canadian Politics* (Toronto: McGraw-Hill Ryerson, 1975); John Klein, "Habitual Offender Legislation and the Bargaining Process," *The Criminal Law Quarterly*, 15 (April, 1974), pp. 2-18.

46 Marchak, *Ideological Perspectives on Canada*, p. 51.

is to protect the public interest in economic competition through prohibiting various types of restraint of trade. Specifically, it is the Department of Consumer and Corporate Affairs' role "to assist in maintaining free and open competition . . . in a system of free enterprise."[47] The traditional concern of the laws formulated and enacted by the federal government has been explicitly stated as providing for the "health and safety of the bodies and minds of the people who compose society."[48]

Method of Study

The object of this study is to partially replicate, in a Canadian context, Edwin H. Sutherland's classic study on corporate crime in the United States, *White Collar Crime*.[49] We will approach the subject area from the conflict perspective. It is to Sutherland's credit that, in a book published twenty-five years prior to his undertaking his study on white-collar crime, he had realized the significance of understanding the origin, administration and enforcement of the legal system in order to achieve an understanding of crime: "An understanding of the nature of criminal law is necessary in order to secure an understanding of the nature of crime. A complete explanation of the origin and enforcement of laws would be, also, an explanation of the violation of laws."[50]

Sutherland clearly believed that the violations of the laws were just as abundant among individuals of the upper socioeconomic class in the United States as they were among members of the lower socioeconomic class, a fact which was not evident in the official crime statistics at that time.[51] Noting that the study of criminology was confined to a limited area of inquiry by criminologists, specifically to those individuals defined as "criminal" by the legal system, it was Sutherland's intention to bring into proper focus the magnitude of

---

47 Donald Mitchell, *The Politics of Food* (Toronto: James Lorimer and Company, 1975), p. 169.

48 Bob McDonald, "Criminality and the Canadian Anti-Combines Law," *Alberta Law Review*, 9 (1965), pp. 67-95. The power to regulate in the "public interest" at the federal level came from section 91 of the British North America Act.

49 Edwin H. Sutherland, *White Collar Crime* (New York: Holt, Rinehart and Winston, 1959).

50 Edward H. Sutherland, *Criminology* (Philadelphia: J. B. Lippincott, 1924), p. 11.

51 This difference still exists in government crime statistics today in Canada, as well as other countries. For information concerning Canada, see William McGrath, *Crime and Its Treatment in Canada* (Toronto: Macmillan, 1965). See also, Robert Silverman and James Teevan, eds., *Crime in Canadian Society* (Scarborough: Butterworth and Company, 1975).

criminal activity which occurred daily by uncovering the criminality of businessmen in their role as corporate executives. Earlier research by Sutherland in 1940 and 1941 dealing with unethical business practices suggested to him that the legal system considered such actions to be violations of civil rather than criminal law. Consequently, the courts dealt with "smalltime" thieves in a harsh manner, often sending the convicted to prison for an extended term to deter and rehabilitate him and to protect society. In comparison, businessmen who frequently defrauded the public to a greater degree were assessed insignificant fines. Yet Sutherland pointed out that these crimes by businessmen—white-collar crimes—were the most economically dangerous to the well-being of society. This discretionary bias in the criminal justice system was a direct result of politicians, judges and others being "culturally homogeneous" with businessmen, and thus being willing to accommodate businessmen's powerful interest groups which wanted to avoid the social stigma and penal sanctions imposed under criminal law. The result was that criminal acts committed by businessmen were treated as violations of civil rather than criminal law due to the special legislation passed by the state in order to protect them.

Special procedures constructed by the government led to the criminality of businessmen being "blurred", "concealed", and "not made specific". Although various mechanisms were used to enforce the antitrust laws by considering criminal acts by corporate executives as either violations of criminal or civil law (with emphasis upon the latter), it was Sutherland's contention that many violations of the antitrust laws were *criminal* acts and should be treated as such. He wrote that such procedures "are based on decisions that a criminal law was violated and therefore that a crime was committed; the decisions of a civil court or a court of equity as to these violations are as *good evidence of criminal behaviour as is the decision of a criminal court*" [emphasis added].[52] Sutherland proposed to investigate these criminal acts, his thesis being that:

Persons of the upper socio-economic class engage in much criminal behaviour; that criminal behaviour of the lower socio-economic class differed principally in administrative procedures which are used in dealing with the offenders, and that variations in administrative procedures are not significant from the point of view of causation of crime.[53]

In his study of the seventy largest industrial and mercantile corporations in the United States, Sutherland revealed that they had been

---

52 Sutherland, *White Collar Crime*, p. 22.
53 *Ibid.*, p. 34.

investigated by the government for violating various antitrust laws a total of 980 times, and only 158 (or 16%) of these violations had been dealt with by the courts as criminal offences. He did not concern himself with the conviction rate of corporations which would have been much lower than the figures presented here. Sutherland pointed out that not all of these unlawful actions committed by the corporate executives were criminal and, as such, "these decisions can be used as a measure of criminal behaviour only in so far as the other 822 decisions can be shown to be decisions that the behaviour was *criminal* as well as unlawful" [emphasis added].[54]

Sutherland approached the study of white-collar crime according to the tenets of the order approach. What he had done was to embark on his study from a sociopsychological perspective: he asked why certain *individuals* became involved in criminal activities while others did not. "White collar crimes may be defined approximately as a crime committed by a *person* of respectability and high social status in the course of his occupation" [emphasis added].[55] The order perspective focuses on the actions of the individual, viewing the state as a given, beyond any incrimination whatsoever, serving the needs of the people by maintaining a stable society. The law and its agents of enforcement are also viewed as "neutral" and as mediators in the conflicts of society. Most of the studies of corporate crime have emphasized "kinds of people" and/or "kinds of environment" explanations for the illegal behaviour.[56]

The conflict perspective, however, treats as problematic what Sutherland and many others assumed as a given, namely the state and its legal order. We need to treat the state and the origin, administration and enforcement of its laws as problematic, and not as a given. Such an approach calls for a reinterpretation of the area of study for the discipline of criminology. Students of crime taking the conflict perspective believe that the traditional restriction of criminology to

---

54 Herman Schwendinger and Julia Schwendinger, "Defenders of Order or Guardians of Human Rights?" *Issues in Criminology*, 5 (Summer, 1970), p. 9.

55 *Ibid.*, p. 9.

56 Geis, *White Collar Criminal*; William N. Leonard and Marvin Glenn Weber, "Automakers and Dealers: A Study of Criminogenic Market Factors," *Law and Society Review* 4 (February, 1970), pp. 407-24; Don C. Gibbons, *Society, Crime and Criminal Careers*, 2nd Edition (Englewood Cliffs: Prentice-Hall, Inc., 1973), pp. 325-53; Harvey A. Farberman, "A Criminogenic Market Structure: The Automobile Industry," *Sociological Quarterly*, 16 (Autumn, 1975), pp. 438-57; Barry M. Slow and Eugene Szwajkowiski, "The Scarcity-Munificence Component of Organizational Environments and the Commission of Illegal Acts," *Administrative Science Quarterly*, 20 (September, 1975), pp. 345-54; G. Rosenbluth and H. Thorburn, *Canadian Anti-Combines Legislation 1952-1960* (Toronto: University of Toronto Press, 1963).

individuals and/or their environment is insufficient for understanding crime in society. It is necessary to surpass the limits of such traditional criminology and to focus upon those social relationships formed by the political, social and economic powers which have a direct say in what is thought to be criminal in our society. Taylor, *et al.*, point out that by approaching criminology within this framework, a profound change is experienced by criminology: "A criminology which is adequate to an understanding of these developments and which will be able to bring politics back into the discussion of what was previously technical issues will need to deal with society as a totality."[57] Concerning white-collar crime in general and corporate crime specifically, a power/conflict analysis emphasizes a critical analysis of the emergence of laws, their enforcement and administration within the context of dominant interests and elites. Emphasis is placed upon the nature of the nation state, capitalism and the power of elites within society.[58] Such an approach may take us from the study of white-collar crime to the study of exploitation.[59]

It has been suggested by Lehmann and Young that the traditional methods of study used by social scientists have primarily supported and advanced the basic interests of large-scale organizations, to the benefit of "managers, stockholders, and policy makers, at the expense of the interests of blue collar workers, white collar workers, and the public in general."[60] This co-optation by social scientists to powerful state interests has not been limited to the collection of insignificant and isolated data, as the exposés of such state-supported and -controlled research projects, like Project Camelot and the Pentagon Papers, testify. As Platt points out, much criminological research in particular has served and facilitated the interests of state-controlled agencies: "Much criminological research is 'agency-determined' and subordinated to institutional interests, whereby the formation of

---

57 Taylor *et. al., The New Criminology*, p. 278.

58 See Quinney, *Criminology*, pp. 131-45; William Chambliss, "Toward a Political Economy of Crime," *Theory and Society*, 2 (Summer, 1975), pp. 149-70; Bert Young, "Corporate Interests and the State," *Our Generation*, 10 (Winter-Spring, 1975), pp. 70-83.

59 Harold E. Pepinsky, "From White Collar Crime to Exploitation: Redefinition of a Field," *The Journal of Criminal Law and Criminology*, 65 (June, 1974), pp. 225-33.

60 Timothy Lehmann and Ted Young, "From Conflict Theory to Conflict Methodology: An Emerging Paradigm for Sociology," *Sociological Inquiry*, 44 (Winter, 1974), p. 25. For a more recent discussion of conflict methodology see Ted Young, "Some Theoretical Foundations for Conflict Methodology," *Sociological Inquiry*, 46 (Winter, 1976), pp. 23-29.

research problems, the scope of inquiry, and the conditions of funding are determined by the 'agency' rather than by 'scholars'."[61]

This production of narrow and specialized information by criminologists and other social scientists through consensus-based methodologies has relegated the state and big business to "unknown" areas because they are unresearched, even though they have had a significant impact upon the direction and quality of society: "Adherence to the canons of corporate professionalism and consensus methodology make it very difficult for sociologists to investigate large scale organizations and assess their social, political, economic, and psychological impacts on society."[62]

Conflict methodology, in contrast, directs itself to the investigation and uncovering of the interests and powers held by these large-scale organizations. Those methods which direct themselves to collecting "quality information" from these organizations provide a means by which to investigate the government's real intentions compared to their public statements of "protecting the public interest." The vehicle used as the mechanism to investigate and evaluate the government *vis-à-vis* their stated intentions concerning combines legislation are various reports from investigatory bodies and royal commissions, comparing the proposed legislation and the final Act, as well as other administrative and enforcement considerations, such as the nature of penalties, etc. Through the following study we will gain an insight into the actual role of the state in relation to anti-combines legislation.

---

61 Tony Platt, "Prospects for a Radical Criminology in the United States," *Crime and Social Justice*, 1 (Spring-Summer, 1974), p. 4.

62 Lehmann and Young, " "From Conflict Theory to Conflict Methodology," p. 20.

CHAPTER 3

The Emergence of Canadian Anti-Combines Legislation

Legislation was only introduced and amended when class conflict threatened the ruling class; that is, when the petit bourgeoisie felt squeezed out of the competition, or when working class discontent, intensified during periods of economic depression, threatened severe disruption.

Bert Young, "Corporate Interests and the State," *Our Generation* 10 (Winter-Spring, 1974), p. 73.

Previous to 1889, when Canada's first legislation dealing with combines was enacted, British law gave considerable flexibility to businessmen to form combines, trusts and other agreements limiting competition. Agreements of this nature existed in Canada as early as 1855, when the Grand Trunk and Western Railroads fixed freight rates and limited other competitive practices between them.[1] The first case of possible illegal business activity among certain salt manufacturers in Eastern Canada was taken to the courts in 1871, but was held to be within the limits of the law.

With the formulation of the National Policy in 1879 by the Conservative Government, a great number of businesses entered into combines for the purposes of reducing competition and enhancing profits in Canada. This policy included a protectionist tariff which allowed Canadian manufacturers freedom to develop and expand their companies by restricting all related foreign competition. Subsequently, the formation, development and expansion of large industrial concerns, both domestic and foreign, such as Imperial Oil, occurred, as well as a proliferation of trade agreements among smaller manufacturers, wholesalers, and dealers. The most significant of these agreements in terms of the first Canadian combines legislation was the Dominion Wholesale Grocers' Guild, formed in 1884. The objective of the Guild, which accounted for 95% of the grocery trade in Ontario and Quebec at the time, was to form preferential trade agreements with manufacturers of certain foodstuffs, and fix prices among all members to terminate any competition.[2]

In 1887, the Guild arranged to fix the price of sugar, a product which at that time accounted for 40% of the grocery trade. It was this decision which led two grocers, members of the Guild but non-supportive of the sugar agreement, to challenge the validity of this *particular* agreement in the courts.[3] The philosophy behind combines, trusts, and related agreements was not to be contested. Both grocers pursued this matter for personal reasons, not out of concern for the plight of the consumer.[4] The chief complainant, a small businessman, was one of the original members of the Guild, and had been instrumental in originating agreements on certain foodstuffs, even being one

---

1 Michael Bliss, *A Living Profit* (Toronto: McClelland and Stewart Limited, 1974), p. 35.

2 John Ball, *Canadian Anti-Trust Legislation* (Baltimore: The Williams and Wilkins Company, 1934), p. 5.

3 L. A. Skeoch, "Canada," in *Resale Price Maintenance*, ed., Basil S. Yamey (New York: Aldine Publishing Company, 1966), pp. 23-64.

4 Bruce C. McDonald, "Criminality and the Canadian Anti-Combines Laws," *Alberta Law Review*, 9, no. 1 (1965) 69.

of the first members to suggest a price fix on sugar.[5] The thrust of the original criticism of combines came not from the general populace but from small businessmen, who felt their firms were at the mercy of big business interests. It was this group who directly sponsored the first anti-combines legislation.[6]

Greater political concerns faced the Conservative Government. They feared that the National Policy might become the object of a national public controversy initiated by opposition Liberals, who favoured a free trade philosophy. The Liberals believed that combines stemmed directly from the Conservative protectionist philosophy. The Conservative Government, in order to divert attention away from the National Policy, attempted to show that it was concerned about alleviating the economic conditions brought on by combines. It was concerned with maintaining a broad base of support from a "plurality of interest groups",[7] most notably agricultural, which were upset about the rising prices of farm implements occurring as a result of combines. "In the early years the most powerful group opposing businessmen was the agricultural interest—permeated with free trade ideas, stoutly opposed to insolvency that would limit the freedom of debtors, anti-railroad, anti-corporation, and often anti-urban."[8] A Conservative Member of Parliament, Clarke Wallace, acting without government support, first introduced a motion to the House of Commons early in the 1888 session concerning combines. It specifically proposed " . . . a Select Committee be appointed to examine into . . . certain combines said to exist with reference to the purchase and sale, or manufacture and sale, in Canada of any foreign or Canadian products . . . "[9]

Wallace also suggested that the proposed committee, after their investigation, introduce a Bill into the House of Commons which would make "combinations illegal and . . . protect people against high prices."[10] Wallace, a popular consumer advocate and small businessman, was then appointed as the chairperson of the Committee to Investigate and Report upon Alleged Combines in Manufacturers, Trade and Insurance. After two months of investigations into combines,[11] the committee suggested that the government undertake some

---

5 Michael Bliss, "Another Anti-Trust Tradition: Canadian Anti-Combines Policy 1889-1910," in *Enterprise and National Development*, eds., Glenn Porter and Robert D. Cuff (Toronto: Hakkert, 1973), pp. 39-50.

6 Michael Bliss, "Dyspensia of the Mind," in *Canadian Business History*, ed., David Macmillan (Toronto: McClelland and Stewart, 1972), p. 188.

7 *Ibid.*, p. 180.

8 *Ibid.*, p. 180.

9 House of Commons Debates, 1888.

10 Ball, *Canadian Anti-Trust Legislation*, p. 3.

11 The commodities and subjects examined by the Committee were sugar and

form of legislative action to control combines, concluding that: "The Committee finds the evils produced by combinations such as have been inquired into, have not by any means been fully developed as yet in this country, but sufficient evidence of their injurious tendencies and effects is given to justify legislation. . . . "[12]

The overall criticism given by the report on combines was mild, only weakly condemning the actual combines which had been investigated; generally the report was more concerned with the protection of non-members of combines than with protecting consumers from the possible negative effects of them.[13] Wallace proceeded to introduce a *private* member's bill into the House of Commons at a later stage of the 1888 session. Prime Minister Macdonald gave the bill "cautious verbal approval", but alloted it so little time for discussion that it was placed on the next year's agenda for business.[14] The significance of non-sponsorship of the initial legislation in 1888 and in 1889 cannot be underemphasized. Since the bill was Wallace's private doing, the Conservative government "could remain 'neutral' and not endanger" its relations with the larger members of the business community.[15]

Wallace introduced his bill at the beginning of the 1889 session, but once again, the government showed its disinterest by neglecting to

groceries; coal; watch case manufacturers; barbed wire; twine; agricultural implements; stoves; coffin makers, and undertakers; oatmeal millers; egg dealers; barley, and the Canadian Fire Underwriters Association.

12 Report of the Special Committee to Investigate and Report on Alleged Combines in Manufacturers, Trade, and Insurance, 1888.

13 Lloyd Reynolds, *The Control of Competiion in Canada* (Cambridge, Massachusetts: Harvard University Press, 1940), p. 133.

14 House of Commons Debates, 1888; Bill No. 138.

15 The main section of the bill read:
1. Every person who combines, agrees or arranges with any other person, or with any railway, steamship or steamboat or transportation company,
(a) For granting to any person who is a party to such combination, agreement or arrangement any facility for the purchase, sale, transportation or supply of any article or commodity which is an object of trade, which facility is, by such combination, agreement or arrangement, not to be granted to any person who is not a party thereto;
(b) For denying to any person who is not a party to such combination, agreement or arrangement any facility for any such purchase, sale, transportation or supply which, by the provisions thereof, is to be granted to any person who is a party thereto:
(c) For unreasonably enhancing the market price of an article or commodity which is an object of trade;
(d) For unduly restraining the traffic in any such article or commodity;
(e) For limiting, lessening or preventing the production, manufacture, sale or transportation of any such article or commodity;
(f) For preventing or restricting competition in the production, manufacture, sale or transportation of any such article or commodity;
Is guilty of a misdemeanor and liable, on conviction, to a penalty not exceeding one thousand dollars and not less than two hundred dollars, or to imprisonment for any term not exceeding twelve months and not less than three months or to both.

place it on its schedule of business. The bill was referred by the federal government to the Committee on Banking and Commerce, where opponents were able to speak directly to the proposed legislation. As a result of this opportunity, much pressure was put on this committee by business interests, and the bill returned to the House of Commons in a remarkably different form. The provision which stated that upon conviction for an offence a corporation would lose its charter was omitted, as were Section 1, subsections (a) and (b). More importantly for the future enforcement of the bill, the committee added the word "unlawfully" to the end of Section 1; "conspires" was inserted before "combines" in the same section; and "unduly" and "unreasonably" were deleted in subsections 1(c) and 1(d).[16]

Upon second reading of the bill in the House of Commons, the government announced its support—at least ostensibly—for the proposed legislation. Wallace was personally disappointed with the content of the new bill, and blamed strong business lobbies for the changes.[17] Wallace charged that these changes resulted from the pressure of " ... those men who have formed those illegal combinations and who came down ... with a great array of lawyers from Montreal and Toronto and with amendments carefully considered, to legislate the bill out of existence."[18] McDonald notes that these changes stemmed from the committee's belief that the men involved were not criminals, and that the bill in its original form would lead to a "vague prescription of conduct for which a criminal penalty was inappropriate."[19] Following the second reading of the bill, it was sent to the

---

16 House of Commons Debates, 1889; Bill No. 11 [italics added]. As amended by the Committee on Banking and Commerce and presented before the House of Commons, the bill now read:
1. Every person who conspires, combines, agrees or arranges with any other person, or with any railway, steamship, steamboat or transportation company, *unlawfully*,
   (a) To limit the facilities for transporting, producing, manufacturing, supplying, storing or dealing in any article or commodity which may be a subject of trade and commerce; or—
   (b) To restrain or injure trade or commerce in relation to any such article or commodity; or—
   (c) To prevent, limit, or lessen the manufacture or production of any such article or commodity, or to enhance the price thereof; or—
   (d) To prevent or lessen competition in the production, manufacture, purchase, barter, sale, transportation or supply of any such article or commodity, or in the price of insurance upon person or property:
   Is guilty of a misdemeanor and liable on conviction, to a penalty not exceeding four thousand dollars and not less than two hundred dollars, or to imprisonment for any term not exceeding two years; and if a corporation, is liable on conviction to a penalty not exceeding ten thousand dollars and not less than one thousand dollars.
17 House of Commons Debates, April 22, 1889.
18 House of Commons Debates, 1889, quoted in L. G. Reynolds, *The Control ...*, pp. 131-32.
19 McDonald, *Criminality and the Canadian Anti-Combines Laws*, p. 70.

Senate for final approval. The Senate, however, proceeded to change the bill, inserting the word "unduly" in Section 1, subsections (a), (c) and (d), and the word "unreasonably" in Section 1, subsection (c). Wallace and his supporters were opposed to these changes, but decided that an Act with some shortcomings was at least immediately enforceable. It was feared that to debate the Senate amendments would mean at least another year with the law unenforced.[20]

The general belief held by most, if not all, of those directly connected with the new Act, was that it was simply declaratory of the common law. Therefore the Act was assumed to be based upon prior legal precedent. In fact, however, it went far beyond the common law position. For the Crown to prove that an illegal combine had been formed, and be able to convict the parties involved, the word "unlawful" would have to be deleted. At the common law level, there existed no laws dealing with combines formed by businessmen, legal or illegal. Indeed, with the words "unduly" and "unreasonably" placed with "unlawful" in Section 1, the onus was put on the prosecution to show "not only that the common law had been violated, insofar as the offence fell within the statute [which was impossible], but also that trade had been restrained 'unduly'."[21]

The confusion which surrounded the legality of this first legislation dealing with combines was the result of the lawmakers' misinterpretation of the notion of conspiracy upon which combines legislation is based. The first conspiracy statutes in English law appeared in 1293. However, trade among merchants was not strictly regulated by criminal statute until the seventeenth century, and only then were violators

---

20 House of Commons Debate, April 22, 1889. The first, and most important section of the bill, as amended by the Senate and presented to the House of Commons, and finally enacted, read as follows:
1. Every person who conspires, combines, agrees or arranges with any other person, or with any railway, steamship, steamboat or transportation company, *unlawfully*,
 (a) To *unduly* limit the facilities for transporting, producing, manufacturing, supplying, storing or dealing in any article or commodity which may be a subject of trade or commerce; or—
 (b) To restrain or injure trade or commerce in relation to any such article or commodity; or—
 (c) To *unduly* prevent, limit, or lessen the manufacture or production of any such article or commodity, or to *unreasonably* enhance the price thereof; or—
 (d) To *unduly* prevent or lessen competition in the production, manufacture, purchase, barter, sale, transportation or supply of any such article or commodity, or in the price of insurance upon person or property:
Is guilty of a misdemeanor and liable, on conviction, to a penalty not exceeding four thousand dollars and not less than two hundred dollars, or to imprisonment for any term not exceeding two years; and if a corporation, is liable on conviction to a penalty not exceeding ten thousand dollars and not less than one thousand dollars [italics added].
21 Richard Gosse, *The Law on Competition in Canada* (Toronto: The Carswell Company Limited, 1962), p. 73.

punished as criminal offenders.[22] By the middle of the eighteenth century, all conspiracy statutes which dealt with the hindering of free trade on the part of merchants were removed, as the judiciary was amendable to the idea that fixing prices and restricting output were acceptable business practices. "Freedom to trade meant freedom to combine....."[23]

The bulk of the legislation concerning conspiracies in English law prior to the twentieth century dealt with the suppression of trade union activity in the market place. In 1799 and 1800 the House of Commons in England passed combination laws forbidding "agreements by workmen for altering hours, lessening quantity of work, and hindering or controlling masters in the conduct of their business."[24] In 1825, the courts ascertained that charges of conspiracy could be laid against workers disrupting the activities of their employers. "Thus, combinations were prevented from obtaining an increase in wages by the use of coercion. The use of the strike as a weapon in trade disputes remained illegal."[25] The situation in which trade unions were considered unlawful associations existed until 1871, when the Trade Union Act established their legality.

If this first piece of combines legislation in Canada did not declare the common law, then what was the source of this misunderstanding? One explanation was that no one was aware of the position of the common law at the time.[26] Another possibility was that the government was quite aware that Wallace's original bill could have far-reaching implications on business practices; indeed, until the Committee on Banking and Commerce amended it by introducing the word "unlawful"—which made the proposed legislation meaningless—the government did not offer its support of the bill. With all possible problems aside the government could then appear to the public as protectors of their rights and, at the same time, privately inform "their supporters in the business community that there was nothing for them to worry about."[27] The Canadian Minister of Justice, Sir John Thompson, also believed that the bill was declaratory of the common law. His erroneous interpretation resulted from his reliance upon the interpretation of the leading English authority on the subject, Sir William Earle, whose information was based upon the law as it existed in 1869. At

---

22 Ian Wahn, "Canadian Law of Trade Combinations" (Part I). *The Canadian Law Review* 23, no. I (January, 1945), pp. 10-34.

23 Gosse, *Law on Competition in Canada*, p. 18.

24 Wahn, *Canadian Law of Trade Combinations*, p. 18.

25 Gosse, *Law on Competition in Canada*, p. 22.

26 *Ibid.*, pp. 37-39.

27 *Ibid.*, p. 68.

this time, however, English law did not recognize a conspiracy to obstruct trade except in the context of labour unions and this led to the misunderstanding of the first business Combines Law in Canadian legal history.[28]

The ineffectiveness of Canada's first combines legislation is evidenced by the fact that *no permanent enforcement agency was set up at the federal level* which would administer the various provisions. Enforcing the Act fell upon the provincial attorneys general, whose hesitancy to enforce this legislation led to the active and public growth of combines. For example, a combine between salt distributors was formed early in 1889; the Canadian Packers' Association formed later in the year to organize and fix prices of the new crop of fruits and vegetables; and the Dominion Wholesale Grocers' Guild, the same organization which had led to Wallace's initial bill, continued to function in the same capacity as it had before.[29]

This weak legislation concerning combines illustrates the Conservative Government's belief that the National Policy and its tariff walls were sufficient to maintain a free market system in Canada. "... at this stage it was hardly necessary for the government to supplement the operations of the free market with legislation. The very operation of the free market was both a symptom of ... business disunity ... and a guarantee that it would continue to exist."[30]

The National Policy, however, was not creating a solid industrial base controlled by indigenous manufacturers. It was simply putting a tariff solely on imported goods. Foreign investment, especially from the United States, was actively encouraged, with the result that branch plants of large U.S. corporations were started, most notably Standard Oil, American Tobacco Company, and the United Shoe Company Limited. Faced with such competition, domestic manufacturers, with their weak capital base, could not compete. Even though the National Policy was seemingly implemented to benefit the growth of a new Canadian Manufacturing era, the Conservatives "preferred to import 'wholesale' an industrial system from the U.S. rather than support nascent entrepreneurs already present ... it chose to dominate and contain them ... by moving in and consolidating industrially-based entrepreneurial firms into joint stock complexes...."[31]

Large Canadian financiers soon began to take over control of

28 *Ibid.*, pp. 38-39.
29 Bliss, *A Living Profit*, pp. 36, 39.
30 Bliss, "Dyspensia of the Mind," p. 188
31 Wallace Clement, *The Canadian Corporate Elite* (Toronto: McClelland and Stewart Ltd., 1975), p. 66.

many small but viable Canadian industries,[32] not out of "communal or vocational interest",[33] but in the interests of immediate profits, buying and selling them like pieces of stock. Soon, there emerged large concentrated manufacturing concerns out of the consolidation of these small manufacturing concerns. For example, the Steel Company of Canada was formed in such a manner by finance capitalists.[34]

As these large industrial concerns began to develop and flourish, Wallace proposed amendments to the Act in both 1891 and 1892, suggesting the omission of the words "unreasonably" and "unduly" rather than the strategic word "unlawfully". Both times his proposals were defeated, as members of parliament felt that the deletion of the two words would result in *all* combinations being prosecuted, even those considered to be supportive of the public interest.

In 1892, the Act was placed in the Criminal Code as Sections 516, 517, and 520 with no substantial changes occurring in its intent or application.[35] When the Liberals formed the government in 1897, they proposed a bill which would penalize members of illegal combines by removing tariffs,[36] thereby inducing competition for the benefit of the Canadian consumer. This bill became known as the Customs Tariff Act, and it led to a successful conviction of members of a paper

---

32 T. W. Acheson, "The National Policy and the Industrialization of the Maritimes, 1880-1919," *Acadensis* I (Spring 1977).

33 Acheson, *ibid.*, pp. 23-24.

34 Clement, *The Canadian Corporate Elite*, p. 69.

35 The relevant sections read:
516. A Conspiracy in restraint of trade is an agreement between two or more persons to do or procure to be done any unlawful act in restraint of trade.
517. The purposes of a trade union are not, by reason merely that they are in restraint of trade, unlawful within the meaning of the next preceding section. R.S.C., c. 131, s. 22.
520. Every one is guilty of an indictable offence and liable to a penalty not exceeding four thousand dollars and not less than two hundred dollars, or to two years imprisonment, and if a corporation is liable to a penalty not exceeding ten thousand dollars and not less than one thousand dollars, who conspires, combines, agrees or arranges with any other person, or with any railway, steamship, steamboat or transportation company, unlawfully—
   (a) to unduly limit the facilities for transporting, producing, manufacturing, supplying, storing or dealing in any article or commodity which may be a subject of trade or commerce; or—
   (b) restrain or injure trade or commerce in relation to any such article or commodity; or—
   (c) to unduly prevent, limit, or lessen the manufacture or production of any such article or commodity, or to unreasonably enhance the price thereof; or—
   (d) to unduly prevent or lessen competition in the production, manufacture, purchase, barter, sale, transportation or supply of any such article or commodity, or in the price of insurance upon person or property.

36 The Liberals had, since 1888, favoured tariff removal as a penalty and deterrent for all problems of combination and monopoly. See Bliss, *Living Profit*, pp. 44, 50.

combine; the penalty was a reduction of 40% on related American paper imports.[37]

Non-enforcement of the combines legislation continued. In 1899, a Senator Sproule realized the difficulty of prosecuting members of combines for conspiring "unlawfully" to practise certain restraint of trade "unduly". He introduced a motion which would strike out the word "unlawfully"; subsequently, when the motion was passed, the Act suddenly became enforceable under the Criminal Code.[38] Conspiracy to act "unduly" now became an indictable offence. " . . . the parties to conspiracy, etc., could no longer justify a restraint of trade by showing that it was reasonable in reference to their interests and consistent with the interests of the public."[39] Bliss has discussed how this important change originated:

Incredible as it seems, this happened by accident when a Senator, who prided himself on his drafting ability, suggested omitting the word in order to get rid of the 'surplusage' in the section, wording which 'as a matter of art, ought not to prevail.' He was not practicing duplicity, for a few weeks later he explicitly defended the right of combination and the need to keep 'unduly' and 'unreasonably' in the law.[40]

In 1900, the combines legislation was changed to Sections 494-498 of the Criminal Code. The legal significance of this change was not realized until 1903, when provincial attorneys general undertook action against the members of five combines, ultimately leading to the conviction of three.[41] Most of this activity was directed toward the large American corporations.[42] While this "surge" in court actions did not reduce the number of illegal combines, it did make members treat their agreements in a more clandestine manner and become more aware of the legal restraints on their combines.[43] Combines contined to exist, with the Dominion Wholesale Grocers' Guild still playing an active role. "In 1906 a prosecution for conspiracy was brought against the Guild under the combines section of the Criminal Code. Four years later it was acquitted and went on into World War I stabilizing the trade in its usual way."[44]

---

37 Ball, *Canadian Anti-Trust Legislation*, pp. 14-17.

38 Gosse, *Law on Competition in Canada*, pp. 75-76.

39 A. C. Crysler, *Restraint of Trade and Labour* (Toronto: Butterworths, 1967), p. 19.

40 Bliss, "Another . . . Anti-Combines Policy," pp. 45-46.

41 Reynolds, *The Control of Competition in Canada*, p. 136.

42 Bliss, *A Living Profit*, p. 46.

43 *Ibid.*, p. 39.

44 *Ibid.*, p. 34.

CHAPTER 4

The Merger Movement, Mackenzie King and Combines Legislation

It is clear... King, not withstanding his militant posture in Parliament, had no serious intentions about mergers... his half-hearted approach... [was] reflected in the very vagueness and redundancy in which the relevant clauses of his legislation were cloaked.

W. G. Phillips, "Canadian Combines Policy—The Matter of Mergers," *The Canadian Bar Review*, 42, no. I (March, 1964), p. 80.

A merger movement occurred in Canadian industry during the late stages of the first decade in the twentieth century. This "movement" lasted five years, with the result that many small companies merged to form one monopolistic company in almost complete control of a specified industrial sector.[1] At the same time, the cost of living was increasing, and many Canadians blamed these mergers for increased prices of consumer goods and building materials, while their wages remained stable.[2] "The large number of industrial mergers, trade association activities and the wide publicity given to monopoly evils... during these years was a stimulus for reform."[3] It was quite evident that the Criminal Code was not satisfactory in regulating combines. Provincial attorneys general were hesitant to use the Criminal Code to protect the public from increased prices because it was a criminal statute and they didn't want to "prosecute a combination formed in good faith even though it might be breaking the law."[4] Even when provincial attorneys general attempted to enforce combines laws, their efforts often went for naught. When the Superior Court of Quebec convicted the United Shoe Machinery Company for illegally restraining trade, the decision was overturned by the Judicial Committee of the Privy Council, which suggested that new legislation—rather than litigation—was needed to make the combines laws effective.[5]

The Liberal Prime Minister, Laurier, appointed Mackenzie King, then Minister of Labour, to alleviate the political tension created by public unrest by proposing new legislation which could lead to better enforcement. King's own belief concerning government restriction of businessmen's activities was that businesses should be allowed to grow generally unhindered, though at times the government should protect consumers if there was evidence of a blatant misuse of power on the part of large-scale organizations. He also stated that "amalgamation of business units... is in most cases beneficial"[6] to the Canadian economy in competing at the international level.

------

1 J. C. Weldon, "Consolidations in Canadian Industry 1900-1948," in *Restrictive Trade Practices in Canada*, ed., L. A. Skeoch (Toronto: McClelland and Stewart Limited, 1966), pp. 228-79. According to Weldon's figures, 196 firms were reduced to eighty-five during this five-year period (p. 233). See also Wallace Clement, *The Canadian Corporate Elite* (Toronto: McClelland and Stewart, 1975), p. 77; L. Reynolds, *The Control of Competition in Canada* (Cambridge, Massachusetts: Harvard University Press, 1940), p. 68; and T. Naylor, *History of Canadian Business*, Vol. 2 (Toronto: James Lorimer and Co., 1975), p. 187.

2 See Naylor, *ibid.*, p. 187.

3 J. Ball, *Canadian Anti-Trust Legislation* (Baltimore: The Williams and Wilkins Company, 1934), p. 37.

4 *Ibid.*, p. 37.

5 See Naylor, *History of Canadian Business*, p. 193.

6 Reynolds, *The Control of Competition in Canada*, p. 137.

King understood well the implications of using a criminal statute to regulate businessmen. In the parliamentary debates of 1910 concerning combines, King stated:

I think I have shown the House that the legislation of 1889 has not been effective in dealing with the evil of trusts and combines, but that, on the contrary, its real effect in some cases has been to prevent investigation which would otherwise have taken place. The necessity of branding as <u>*criminals any body of men joined together for commercial purposes*</u> <u>*before you find out whether or not they have been guilty of a criminal*</u> <u>*offence, is a step which many a man will hesitate to take, no matter what*</u> <u>*grounds he will have for believing such men to be guilty of a public*</u> <u>*wrong.*</u> *There is no doubt that this necessity has prevented many an investigation which would have been in the interests of the public*[7] [emphasis added].

Another weakness with the enforcement of the Act was that the provincial attorneys general were reluctant to undertake prosecution measures, and as a result the onus was placed upon the complainant to secure evidence of the combination. Such a process was lengthy, time-consuming, and expensive for an individual, and so this avenue for prosecution lay dormant.[8]

King was personally not overly concerned with the public unrest about rising prices, but believed something should be done—not because great trusts and combines were at fault, but because the public had incorrectly judged these trusts to be the source of inflation. There was also the added incentive for King to protect those same trusts which " . . . contributed so much to Liberal party campaign coffers."[9] Anything that he introduced to regulate mergers and combines was for the Liberal "party's own good, to protect them against 'being wrongfully judged by the public'."[10] To absolve the Liberal party's policies from blame for the increasing cost of living, King identified the "extravagances of the wealthy" and the "natural causes" of inflation as the real reasons.[11] King was also determined to avoid pursuing the policies of the Sherman Anti-Trust Laws at that time, as the American courts were vigorously enforcing the law under the interpre-

---

7 House of Commons Debates 1909-1910, IV, p. 6843.

8 W. L. M. King, "The Canadian Combines Investigation Act," *Annals of American Academy of Political and Social Sciences*, Vol. 42 (July, 1912), p. 98.

9 Naylor, *History of Canadian Business*, p. 193.

10 Phillips, *Canadian Combines Policy*, p. 79.

11 House of Commons Debates, IV, p. 6819.

tation that every contract in restraint of trade was illegal.[12]

I have tried to show that this legislation is not brought in with a view to aiming at the formation of combinations as such, but rather a controlling of their actions, so that they may not unduly embarrass or interfere with the rights of the general public. We have sought to avoid the errors which have exhibited themselves in the legislation of other countries. We have tried to avoid the error which the United States have experienced in going too far in one direction, and on the other hand, to avoid being drawn into another extreme position such as has been found in the operation of legislation in Australia[13] [emphasis added].

The Bill which was introduced by King in 1910 (and, after passage, became known as the Combines Investigation Act) was not intended to legislate against combinations that the judiciary considered to be beneficial to the public interest. King made this point clear in speaking to the bill: "This legislation is in no way aimed against trusts, combines and mergers as such, but rather only at the possible wrongful use or abuse of their power, of which certain of these combinations may be guilty."[14]

The new legislation featured provisions relating to investigation and publicity. King's opinion was that publicity would be a sufficient deterrent; if not, a fine of up to $1000 a day would be charged to the guilty parties. The procedure for investigation was elaborate and efficient, at least on paper. Upon the receipt of an application[15] from six or more persons who were residents of Canada and British subjects, a judge would schedule, within the next thirty days, a meeting between the complainants and the "defendants". At the conclusion of the meeting, the judge had the power to order an investigation,[16] demand more information before proceeding, or to refuse to further the investigation. If the judge felt that the evidence warranted an investigation, the Minister of Labour would be informed, and an *ad hoc* board

---

12 This interpretation of the American Sherman Anti-Trust Laws lasted from 1904 to 1911.

13 *House of Commons Debates*, IV, p. 6837.

14 *Ibid.*, p. 6823.

15 The application had to be accompanied by a written statement pointing out how the alleged combine operated to the detriment of the public.

16 Section 7 of the Combines Investigation Act read: "If upon such hearing the judge is satisfied that there is reasonable ground for believing that a combine exists which is injurious to trade or which has operated to the detriment of consumers or producers, and that it is in the public interest that an investigation should be held, the judge shall direct an investigation under the provisions of this Act."

would be appointed. This board would be comprised of one representative each from both the groups of residents and defendants, and a
third member to be agreed upon by the two other members. If the
subsequent investigation found the defendants guilty of a violation,
penalties were restricted only to their conduct *persisted in after* the
report.[17] Penalties were thus attached only to those parties continuing
in a combine, and would amount to a maximum fine of $1000 a day.
In addition, the new Act stipulated that only *collusive* arrangements to
combine were illegal, allowing the individual manufacturer, supplier,
and retailer to restrict trade beyond the constraints of the Act. A new
clause stated that the fixing of prices might lead to a conviction for
injuring the public. King disagreed with the suggestion that an official
investigatory body be established and a permanent commission be
appointed to regulate and enforce the Act.

The introduction of the Combines Investigation Act did not
replace the Criminal Code provisions for combines. Rather, King
hoped that the new Act would deter unlawful practices; but the
Criminal Code could be implemented if the guilty parties did not
discontinue their activities. It was hoped, then, that with the Anti-
Combines Act and the Criminal Code supplementing each other,
monopolistic situations would be avoided in the future.

King included mergers with monopolies and trusts in his Anti-
Combines Act, under the definition of combines, but stated in the
House of Commons that " ... in introducing this legislation, no
attempt is being made to legislate against combines, mergers, and
trusts.... "[18] The new Act now read:

*'Combine' means any contract, agreement, arrangement or combination
which has, or is designed to have, the effect of increasing or fixing the
price or rental of any article of trade or commerce or the cost of the
storage or transportation thereof, or of the restricting competition in or
of controlling the production, manufacture, transportation, storage, sale
or supply thereof, to the detriment of consumers or producers of such
article of trade or commerce, and includes the acquisition, leasing or
otherwise taking over, or obtaining by any person to the end aforesaid, of
any control over or interest in the business, or any portion of the
business, of any other person, and also includes what is known as a trust,
monopoly or merger[19] [emphasis added].*

---

17 As stated in Section 23 of the Combines Investigation Act.
18 House of Commons Debates, April 12, 1910, p. 6803.
19 Section II, part (c), Combines Investigation Act, 1910.

Thus, mergers, monopolies, and trusts were all considered without distinction as one form of the larger category of combines.

The number of mergers during the next two years declined, although a total of twenty-seven mergers accounted for the consolidation of eighty-one firms. Some of the largest—and most concentrated—Canadian manufacturers continued to merge following the new Act. Canadian Consolidated Felt Company gained complete control of the Canadian footware market for one of its subsidiaries in 1911.[20] Other manufacturing areas which increased in concentration after the 1910 legislation included the milling, meat packing, rolling stock and foundry industries.

... Public policy was little more than incantation. The anti-combines act ... was ... transformed into a hotch-potch of sunny banalities. The Act was aimed at the abuses of oligopoly power, not oligopoly per se ... such undue abuses of corporate powers were apparently rare indeed: The Act was never enforced.... [21]

"... Mr. King, notwithstanding his militant posture ... had no serious intentions against mergers in 1910 ... his half-hearted approach being reflected in the very vagueness and redundancy in which the relevant clauses of his legislations were cloaked."[22]

The First World War brought on an increased cost of living and a product shortage to the Canadian public. Charges of "profiteering" and unfair business practices were directed towards various elements of the business community, and in late 1916, an Order in Council was enacted to investigate the rise in the cost of living. The legislation controlled the amount of goods a business or individual held, as well as the price at which such articles could be sold. The Minister of Labour was given special powers to investigate any suspected violation, and the case might be turned over to the applicable provincial attorney general for prosecution if the evidence so permitted. Penalties included a fine not exceeding five thousand dollars, a possible two-year term of imprisonment, or both fine and imprisonment. No record exists of any convictions, and doubts have been raised as to whether any prosecution procedures were initiated.[23] In February 1918, the War Trade Board was established which ultimately would have had complete control over the Canadian economy if the war had continued. "... these boards and agencies dealt with the procurement, allo-

---

20 Naylor, *History of Canadian Business*, pp. 90-191.
21 *Ibid.*, p. 193.
22 Phillips, *Canadian Combines Policy*, p. 80.
23 Reynolds, *The Control of Competition in Canada*, p. 140.

cation, and rationing of scarce materials, and here their greatest successes were scored. Their greatest failure lay in the attempt to control prices, which,... because of the government's own inflationary policies, kept... rising."[24]

The end of World War I did not bring general price reductions on consumer articles, and the public demanded that the government enact legislation to keep inflation in check.[25] Government concern over public discontent caused by unemployment and labour unrest—especially the 1919 general strike in Winnipeg—led to the appointment of a Special Committee to investigate the causes of the current inflation. While the Committee found no excessive state of profiteering, its proposals had far-reaching implications for combines legislation. Their recommendation was that a special tribunal board be established, with power not only to investigate mergers, trusts, and monopolies, but also to ensure fair prices.[26] The bills implementing the recommendations were presented in Parliament soon after, leading to the establishment of the Board of Commerce Act and the Combines and Fair Prices Act. From the Board of Commerce Act a permanent board for investigation was set up—the Board of Commerce—consisting of three members, Judge H. A. Robson, Mr. W. F. O'Connor, a lawyer, and Mr. James Murdock, a trade union official. They were responsible for the administration of the Combines and Fair Prices Act. This Board was given judicial powers for conducting its investigations, and its decision on any case was to be binding and conclusive. While the definition of combines remained the same as in the 1910 Act, the question of whether or not a combine was functioning to the detriment of the public was to be decided *solely* by the Board.[27] If the Board found evidence of a combine, they would issue a cease and desist order, violation of which was an indictable offence. "The entire anti-combine machinery was thus centralized in the hands of three individuals."[28] A second function of the Board was that it could also determine a fair price for an article in question, compel the owners not only to sell at that price, but also to sell a designated amount of their stock at that price.

During its lifespan the Board received few formal complaints, but

---

24 Donald Creighton, *Canada's First Century* (Toronto: The Macmillan Company of Canada Limited, 1970), p. 138.

25 *Ibid.*, p. 138.

26 These two interpretations were both included within the definition of combines, Section 2, Combines and Fair Prices Act. The fair price section was designed to prevent hoarding and undue enhancement of prices in the "necessaries of life."

27 Reynolds, *The Control of Competition in Canada*, p. 142.

28 *Ibid.*, p. 142.

was very active, based upon its own initiative. Almost all of the Board's activity was directed toward the fair prices section, leaving the combines aspect almost completely dormant. In the first six months of its existence, the Board issued fifty orders to cease and desist under the fair prices section, and made more than seventy-five decisions, most concerned with retailers rather than manufacturers.[29] Representations were made by retailers to the government concerning the Board's powers, and internal strife and political intervention also plagued the Board.[30] The chairperson of the Board resigned early in 1920, and the other two members followed four months later; as such, the Board ceased to function. Mr. Murdock, in his letter of resignation, charged that the government had never been sympathetic with the Acts, and had only recommended their passage due to the alarm caused by the Winnipeg General Strike. He also accused the government of appointing a "safe" man and of Cabinet interference in the Board's business.[31] The constitutional validity of these Acts was ultimately brought before the Supreme Court of Canada in 1921. After the Supreme Court divided equally upon the question, the Judicial Committee of the Privy Council declared these statutes to be *ultra vires*.[32] The Board of Commerce was thus seen as emergency economic legislation rather than a long-term piece of legislation in combines control.[33]

The Privy Council's decision in November 1921 effectively eliminated all Canadian anti-combines legislation.[34] Indeed, anti-combines legislation between 1889 and 1920 had little, if any, impact upon business activities. While the Criminal Code was an alternative after 1900, no administrative machinery had been organized to investigate complaints and possibly start prosecution procedures. The 1910 Combines Investigation Act's procedure for hearing complaints had proven so costly and lengthy for the average citizen that it generally remained unused. And while the 1919 Board of Commerce was a permanent board, its powers proved to be too broad as it was able to enforce the Criminal Code with no restrictions either from Parliament or the judiciary, thereby leading to its being declared non-constitutional. Spe-

---

29 V. Bladen, *An Introduction to Political Economy*, 2nd ed. (Toronto: University of Toronto Press, 1951), p. 218.

30 Reynolds, *The Control of Competition in Canada*, p. 144.

31 House of Commons Debates, 1921, pp. 3603-7.

32 R. Gosse, *The Law on Competition In Canada*. (Toronto: Carswell, 1962), pp. 226-27.

33 D. G. Blair, "Combines, Control, or Competition?" *The Canadian Bar Review*, 36, No. 10 (December, 1953), p. 1093.

34 While the Criminal Code statutes remained valid, it was necessary to get the Board of Commerce's approval to proceed with a prosecution; as no Board existed, permission could not be received.

cifically, it was that section of the Act which gave the Board the power to determine fair profits which was declared unconstitutional, as it was held to be interfering with the property and civil rights in the provinces.

A new Combines Investigation Act was passed in 1923 to fill this legislative void. Mackenzie King, now prime minister, personally sponsored the Act, which was essentially a continuation of the 1910 Act. Important additions were made dealing with greater powers for investigation. A permanent registrar's position was set up to administer the Act, and that official could initiate a preliminary inquiry either upon the formal application of six persons—resident in Canada and British subjects—or on a personal decision; the Governor in Council could also initiate an inquiry and would then appoint commissioners, who had the same powers as the registrar.[35] An important difference lay in the fact that prior to this Act the six complainants had to pay for legal costs, etc., and make their identities public; under the provisions of the 1923 Act, their identities were not to be revealed, and the government took immediate control of all legal aspects of the case upon receipt of the application.

Another important change was that if the Minister of Labour felt the evidence collected warranted prosecution and the provincial attorney general in question did not start action, any *citizen* over twenty-one years of age had the right to inform the Solicitor General of Canada. Subsequent instructions would be given to the Minister of Justice to undertake court action against the alleged violator(s).

The legislation introduced new provisions for penalties. If an *individual* was found guilty of an offence, that person was liable to a penalty not exceeding $10 000 or two year's imprisonment; for corporations, a conviction could lead to a maximum $25 000 fine. Other penalties included lowering or abolishing tariffs if an investigation revealed that a combination was abetted by customs duties; as well, a holder of a patent, if proved to have unduly limited manufacture of a product or in any other way restrained trade, etc., would have all patent privileges revoked.

While in the 1910 legislation it was a crime to continue to be a member of a combine after a cease and desist order had been issued, King now made it a crime to agree to assist in the formation of a combine, whether or not that combine had ceased to exist. The Act now stated "every person is guilty of an indictable offence who is party to ... a combine." Not until this provision was enacted, thirty-

---

35 These powers included the right to summon witnesses, examine records, and secure documents.

nine years after the first legislation had been introduced, did the actual process of merging become an offence.[36] While combines were defined in exactly the same way as they had been in the 1910 Act, this new legislation differed in that the criminality of a combine was based upon the opinion of an investigating officer. Convictions would only follow from a prosecution in the courts.

However, the Prime Minister had not changed his views of large-scale organizations. They continued to be, according to King, advantageous to the business sector, so once again this act was directed to those who improperly used their powers. In the 1923 debates, King reiterated his 1910 philosophy, "The legislation does not seek in any way to restrict just combinations or agreements between business and industrial houses and firms, but it does seek to protect the public against the possible ill effects of these combinations."[37]

King also retained the provisions of publicity as a deterrent to possible offenders—prevention rather than prosecution was once again to be emphasized.

The value of a measure of this kind is not to be estimated by the number of prosecutions that take place, nor by the number of investigations. Rather is it to be estimated by the power of prevention which lies in the fact that it is known that a certain course of procedure will inevitably lead to an investigation and disclosure of conduct that is contrary to the public interest.[38]

The Act itself was passed in June 1923,[39] and enforcement activity under the Act was greater than before, but then so were the possible violations of the Combines Act. During the five-year period between

---

36 Phillips, *Canadian Combines Policy*, p. 81.
37 House of Commons Debates, 1923, III, p. 2520.
38 *Ibid.*, p. 2605.
39 In this Act, unless the context otherwise requires,
(1) combines which have operated or are likely to operate to the detriment or against the interest of the public, whether consumers, producers or others, and which (a) are mergers, trusts or monopolies, so called; or (b) result from the purchase, lease, or other acquisition by any person of any control over or interest in the whole or part of the business of any other person; or (c) result from any actual or tacit contract, agreement, arrangement, or combination which has or is designed to have the effect of (i) limiting facilities for transporting, producing, manufacturing, supplying, storing or dealing, or (ii) preventing, limiting or lessening manufacture or production, or (iii) fixing a common price or resale price, or a common rental, or a common cost of storage or transportation, or (iv) enhancing the price, rental or cost of article, rental, storage or transportation, or (v) preventing or lessening competition in, or substantially controlling within any particular area or district or generally, production, manufacture, purchase, barter, sale, storage, transportation, insurance or supply, or (vi) otherwise restraining or injuring trade or commerce, as described by the word "combine."

1925 and 1930, 231 consolidations were recorded, joining some of the largest Canadian firms together. These large Canadian interests had not reached their dominant position by growth alone, but by a merger or a history of merging activity.[40]

This high level of concentration continued into the Depression which had the effect of eliminating many small firms, reinforcing the dominant position of a few large firms. Reynolds points out that in the 1930s, industrial concentration by control of output was evident in the following manufacturing industries: automobiles, ammunition, cement, cotton yarn and cloth, heavy electrical equipment, lead, meat-packing, tobacco and pulp and paper among others. These concentrated industries earned higher rates of profits than non-concentrated industries during the Depression, earning 12.2% on stockholders' investment, as compared to only 4.0% in the other, non-concentrated industries.[41] "Moreover, concentrated Canadian industries were not hit nearly as hard as others by the Depression. For example, in 1931 their rate of return remained at six per cent while all Canadian manufacturing fell to 1.9 per cent . . . "[42] With the onset of the Depression many people blamed "monopoly" for the economic problems, while businessmen spoke out against the "price cutting" competition and proposed, as an alternative, government controls to limit competition.[43]

It was not until the Conservative party took office in 1931 that a change of philosophy occurred with the Combines Investigation Act. The Conservatives tended to side with businessmen, following a general policy of non-control of combines based upon American experiments with reconstruction of the economy, especially the National Industrial Recovery Act.[44] Combines were no longer regarded as a serious problem, but instead emphasis was on controlling unfair competition, severe competition being considered unfair. Between 1930 and 1935, no reports were published, although some investigations took place.

H. H. Stevens, Minister of Trade and Commerce, assessed combinations of businessmen in favourable terms but denounced the unfair competitive practices and extreme abuses of the marketplace by major chain and department stores and other retailers. He charged that these mass buyers were utilizing their economic power to eliminate smaller retailers, suppliers and producers, and forcing consumers to pay higher

40 See Clement, *Canadian Corporate Elite*, pp. 83-87.
41 Reynolds, *The Control of Competition in Canada*, p. 5.
42 Clement, *Canadian Corporate Elite*, p. 85.
43 Reynolds, *The Control of Competition in Canada*, p. 146.
44 Bladen, *An Introduction to Political Economy*, p. 222.

prices.[45] Stevens had held his policy of "non-intervention" for almost a decade; in the debates over King's Combines Investigation Act in 1923, he had argued:

My chief criticism of the bill is that in effect it declares to be a crime that which is, without question, ordinary, sound business sense. I should also note, with approval the growing tendency of businessmen to eliminate 'vicious' useless competition—such agreements of businessmen improves the efficiency of distribution and stabilizes both prices and production.[46]

By 1934, however, the Conservative Government was in political crisis as the Depression continued, and was in danger of losing almost total public support before the next federal election. Staggering defeats were suffered in that year by provincial Conservative Governments in both Ontario and Saskatchewan, giving a strong indication that the federal party would suffer the next time it went to the polls. The government itself was wracked by internal conflicts concerning the future direction of its economic and social policies, and the party organization was in chaos. That same year Stevens criticized the practices and profits of mass-buying retail outlets, a speech which received national coverage from the mass media. Almost immediately, the public showed their support for Stevens by sending hundreds of letters to the Government outlining the activities of the groups in question. Bennett, attempting to save his party from possible defeat in the next federal election, seized the opportunity to set up a royal commission with Stevens as the chairperson to investigate the marketing of agricultural products, labour conditions, and the buying and selling procedures of chain and department stores. This commission, the Royal Commission on Price Spreads, was granted broad powers to investigate both price spreads in industry and extreme cases of competition.[47] The Commission sat for nearly a year and accumulated a large amount of information in all areas which it investigated.

While the final report presented the "most comprehensive existing treatment of the Canadian economy,"[48] the conclusions of the report were "a strange conglomeration of previous Canadian law and philosophy on the subject of combines, traditional Conservative mistrust of such legislation, American anti-trust experience, and the more recent

45 For a discussion of the impact of mass buying on wage rates, see Reynolds, *The Control of Competition in Canada*, p. 117.

46 House of Commons Debates, 1923, III, p. 2524.

47 Don Mitchell, *The Politics of Food* (Toronto: James Lorimer and Co., 1975), p. 172.

48 Reynolds, *The Control of Competition in Canada*, p. 147.

N.R.A. experiment in the United States."[49] One of the recommendations was for the creation of a Federal Trade and Industry Commission which would have the following seven functions:

i. Rigorous administration of an amended Combines Investigation Act, for the purpose of retaining and restoring competition wherever possible.

ii. Regulation of monopoly in those industries where competition cannot be restored or enforced.

iii. Approval and supervision of agreements regulating prices and production, in industries where competition has proven wasteful or demoralizing.

iv. Prohibition of unfair competitive practices, using methods similar to those of the United States Federal Trade Commission.

v. Administration of existing and proposed laws for the protection of the consumer.

vi. Regulation of new security issues.

vii. Conduct of general economic investigation, and such special inquiries as may be necessary for fulfillment of the above functions. Full publicity was to be given to all findings of the Commission.[50]

The Bill introduced only five of these recommendations, omitting the key proposals concerning the regulation of monopoly and unfair competitive practices. Instead, a new section (498A) was inserted into the Criminal Code. It forbade sellers to discriminate among buyers, to charge different prices in different areas of Canada, or to sell goods at low prices which would lead to the lessening or elimination of competition. This section was ineffective, as no adequate enforcement agencies were established. The legislation became known as the Dominion Trade and Industry Act, establishing a Dominion Trade and Industry Commission, the members of which were given the responsibility for administering the Combines Investigation Act. This Act allowed for the control of prices and production in all industries, but the Commission had the right to veto any such control. The three members of the Commission also composed the Tariff Board, a situation which was termed "deliberate sabotage,"[51] as "its confidential relationship with businessmen unfits it for the role of policemen."[52]

---

49 D. F. Forster, "The Politics of Combines Policy: Liberals and the Stevens Commission," *Canadian Journal of Economics and Political Science*, 28, No. 4 (November, 1962), p. 526.

50 Reynolds, *The Control of Competition in Canada*, p. 147-48.

51 Bladen, *An Introduction to Political Economy*, p. 224.

52 Reynolds, *The Control of Competition in Canada*, p. 224.

A short while later, the Liberal party was returned to power. Mackenzie King, once again prime minister, expressed doubts concerning the validity of the Act because it gave an independent commission the power to define and punish offences without parliamentary sanction.[53] He referred this matter to the Supreme Court for an opinion as to its constitutionality. The Supreme Court, while upholding parts of the Act, held the section legalizing price agreements to be unconstitutional, as it was not related to either criminal law or the regulation of trade and commerce.[54]

The Liberal party then proceeded to restore the Combines Investigation Act to its previous state. In 1937, Mr. N. Rogers, Minister of Labour, introduced amendments intended to restore the old Act to its form of 1923, as well as introducing some new amendments which would strengthen it.[55]

The bill was passed by the House of Commons, and was sent to the Senate for approval, where all the proposed amendments were negated by the Conservative majority. The Conservatives did not support granting to any government department either any powers which could harass business or the right to inflict penalties. The Senators themselves included an amendment which would force the commissioner to seek approval of a judge before an order could be issued or an investigation undertaken. This amendment could result in a delay in the investigation which might lead to the destruction of evidence. Other changes in 1937 allowed for a larger permanent investigative staff; the Commissioner could also, on his personal opinion, request that any report be published. The powers of the Commissioner were restrained also, as an investigation could no longer start on his own initiative, but rather had to wait either for a formal application from six citizens or from directions supplied by the Minister of Labour. The Commissioner was active, starting prosecution procedures six times, but only two resulted in convictions.

---

53 Forster, "Politics of Combines," pp. 519-20.

54 Reynolds, *The Control of Competition in Canada*, pp. 149-50.

55 *Ibid.*, pp. 150-51.

CHAPTER 5

The Politics of Post World War II Combines Revisions

Government and business come together on a number of fronts in Canada but one of the most effective is through the advisory councils and associations . . . created by both business and government . . . . Through these elite forums, and in a variety of other ways, government and industry relate to one another and discover each other's views, form alliances and plan strategies of development not open to the great majority of people . . . . Indeed, it appears the alliance between government and business is not an alliance of equals but one dominated by the interests of corporate capitalism.

Wallace Clement, *The Canadian Corporate Elite* (Toronto: McClelland and Stewart Limited, 1975), pp. 349-50.

During the Second World War, the federal government once again resorted to direct control over the economy, with the Combines Commissioner becoming the Enforcement Administrator of the Wartime Prices and Trade Board. The Wartime Industries Control Board was also established, under the directorship of C. D. Howe. "Each board was vested with dictatorial powers over the direction of Canada's economy."[1] The government allowed the formation of single, large associations, such as the Canadian Wheat Board, to represent a particular industry thinking it easier to obtain maximum production of war materials in this manner instead of dealing with numerous independent competing units.

The Enforcement Administrator, Mr. F. McGregor, was concerned about the government's allowing one large association to represent most firms in crucial industries, as he feared it would make the control of combines more difficult after the war.[2] His investigations into the grocery business after World War II bore out his fears. A survey conducted by him concerning resale price maintenance in this area indicated that while in 1941, 425 items were subject to resale price control, by 1947 this had increased to almost 600 items, an increase of almost 41%.[3]

In 1946, an amendment was passed to the Combines Act which *"restored . . . a provision enabling the Commissioner to proceed on his own initiative with an inquiry to determine whether a combine exists or is being formed"*[4] [italics added]. A further amendment gave the Commissioner power *"to compile information and make studies concerning the existence in Canada of monopolistic conditions"*[5] [italics added]. Thus, the government could not control McGregor's activities, and could be required, by law, to publish all reports submitted. McGregor was very active between 1945 and 1949, with expenditures rising and the number of investigators increasing.[6]

The commissioner or special commissioner who investigated an alleged combine had extensive powers to enter premises, seize documents . . . [H]e then issued a report of his findings, which the law required to be published within fifteen days, whether the government found it agreeable

---

1 Wallace Clement, *The Canadian Corporate Elite* (Toronto: McClelland and Stewart Limited, 1975), p. 88.

2 V. Bladen, *An Introduction to Political Economy*, 2nd ed. (Toronto: University of Toronto Press, 1951), p. 244.

3 Basil S. Yamey, *Resale Price Maintenance* (London: George Weidenfeld and Nicholson Limited, 1966).

4 G. Rosenbluth and H. G. Thorburn, *Canadian Anti-Combines Legislation 1952-1960* (Toronto: University of Toronto Press, 1963), p. 7.

5 *Ibid.*

6 *Ibid.*

or not ... the compulsory publicity was intended to have a puritive effect, and fear of publicity was expected to keep firms from interfering with competition. Thus, there was substance in the charge, often made by business interests, that the commissioner combined the functions of prosecutor and judge. In fact he acted as detective, judge, and then carried out the sentence (by publishing the report).[7]

By the end of 1947, inflation led to public demands for the government to investigate the economic aspects of businessmen's activities. Food prices skyrocketed, for in three weeks

the price of essential food items like meat, cheese, milk and butter rose 20 percent. Prices had increased 135 percent since 1939. Consumer militancy led to demands for re-imposition of wartime price controls. Unions began to demand cost-of-living bonuses as the cost of essentials outstripped average weekly wages. In by-elections in urban Ontario in 1948, the CCF swept to power with a mandate to curb inflation through any means including government take-over.[8]

King's method of appeasing this massive public protest was to use the same tactic for which he had criticized Bennett in 1934: he appointed a parliamentary committee, which proposed such stringent controls as a 25% luxury tax and an excess profits tax. "CCF members were so pleased with the tenor of the report they decided not to submit a minority report."[9] But, two days later, King and the Liberal party formed the Royal Commission on Prices which was to investigate food prices for a year before submitting a final report. Less than half a year later, inflation had levelled off with no formal intervention by the government. King was able to call an election with the political crisis past, and the Liberals won an overwhelming victory, gaining 190 seats in the House of Commons. Part of King's success was that he

moved the focus of investigation as quickly as possible outside the arena of Parliament and parliamentary committees into the judicial inquiry format of a full-time independent Royal Commission. The King government avoided open class divisions and partisan political debate in the process of investigation.[10]

King retired from politics, and Louis St. Laurent and C. D. Howe took over the leadership of the Liberal party. With this change in leadership, a change in anti-combines policy took place. Taking

---

7 *Ibid.*, p. 8.

8 Don Mitchell, *The Politics of Food* (Toronto: James Lorimer and Co., 1975), p. 173.

9 *Ibid.*, p. 173.

10 *Ibid.*, p. 174.

advantage of their intimate relationship with Howe, big business interest groups made suggestions to weaken the Combines Act, and especially to reduce the powers of the Commissioner.

McGregor was very active after World War II, focusing upon
international cartels in manufacturing industries, with the result that
*"large manufacturing firms were ... much more conspicuous among those
investigated than before the war"*[11] [italics added].

In 1949, McGregor submitted a report to the Minister of Justice
concerning a combine in the flour-milling industry which had been in
existence since 1936. Despite the requirement of the combines act that
any report be published by the Minister of Justice fifteen days after its
receipt, more than eleven months passed before it was printed. C. D.
Howe objected to the report, for it criticized the policies of the
Wartime Prices and Trade Board which allowed the flour milling
industry to carry out its activities in such a manner, and many of the
Board's programs had been personally assured by him. "Mr. Howe
made it clear that it was he who urged Mr. Garson [the responsible
minister] 'not to table the report without further investigation.' 'The
full authority of the whole cabinet,' however, supported the delay in
tabling the publication."[12] This inaction led to McGregor's resignation
as Commissioner; in his letter of resignation he called for "an even
stronger statute than the Act in its present form, and a clear statement
of government policy with respect to its enforcement."[13] Also included
was an indictment of the government's attempts to limit the powers of
the Commissioner so he wouldn't upset the practices of large scale
organizations. These attempts came from the Cabinet, and their proposals included eliminating the Commissioner's right to initiate investigations, reducing the number of reports to be made public, and
approving certain business agreements even though they restricted
competition.[14]

The Cabinet's proposals reflected continual business opposition to
anti-combines legislation by attempting to get the government to introduce legal loopholes. The Conservative opposition argued that the
Liberals were not interested in maintaining "free" competition, charging them with breaching the law and seeking to discredit it before the
country.[15]

---

11 Rosenbluth and Thorburn, *Canadian Anti-Combines Legislation*, p. 9.

12 *Ibid.*, p. 13.

13 *Proposals for a New Competition Policy for Canada: First Stage* (Ottawa:
Information Canada, 1973), p. 16A.

14 Rosenbluth and Thorburn, *Canadian Anti-Combines Legislation*, pp. 11-12.

15 H. G. Thorburn, "Pressure Groups in Canadian Politics: Recent Revisions to the
Anti-Combines Legislation," *Canadian Journal of Economics and Political Science*,
30, No. 2 (May, 1964), p. 158.

The problem facing the Liberal party was how to convince the public it was not opposed to the investigation of combines and was genuinely concerned with the public interest while at the same time maintaining close relationships with big business. The government could not, as the protector of the public interest, simply reduce the powers of the Commissioner, so they resolved their difficulty by appointing the Macquarrie Committee[16] to study anti-combines legislation in Canada and other countries. The final report was to recommend possible changes which would make the Combines Investigation Act "a more effective instrument for the encouraging and safeguarding of our free economy."[17] The Committee was also requested to study the issue of resale price maintenance. During the early 1950s, serious inflation once again occurred as a result of the Korean War; the government hoped that the formation of the Macquarrie Committee would alleviate public criticism of the government's policies. "The timing of the legislation and the surrounding circumstances indicate that the main political reason is to be found in the serious inflation that developed in 1950 and 1951, and the resulting public dissatisfaction."[18]

The Committee held open hearings allowing interest groups to express their views. Support for strong anti-combines legislation was voiced by the Consumers' Association of Canada, organized labour and agricultural groups. Both big and small businesses complained of the uncertainties in the existing Act, saying they were at the mercy of the Commissioner's personal interpretations of the various clauses. They sought to decrease the powers of the Commissioner, and limit publication of reports, among other recommendations.[19]

It is evident that most of the recommendations from the business community would have weakened the enforcement of the act by requiring that a specific detriment be proven, reducing the powers of the commissioner, permitting resale price maintenance, and the procedures of judicial enforcement. In contrast, the recommendations of the Canadian Federation of Labour and the Canadian Labour Congress were in favour of strong and effective anti-monopoly action.[20]

After the hearings, the Macquarrie Committee conducted its own investigation, and released its report in two separate sections. The first

---

16 *Ibid.*, p. 159.

17 *Proposals*, p. 22A.

18 G. Rosenbluth and H. G. Thorburn, "Canadian Anti-Combines Administration, 1952-1960," *Canadian Journal of Economics and Political Science*, 27, no. 4 (November, 1961), p. 501.

19 Rosenbluth and Thorburn, *Canadian Anti-Combines Legislation*, pp. 17-25.

20 *Ibid.*, p. 21.

report, issued at the end of 1951, concerned resale price maintenance and proposed that it be made an offence for a supplier to "recommend, prescribe, or enforce minimum resale prices for his products."[21] An amendment to the Combines Investigation Act was passed which made it an offence to fix minimum resale prices. The opposition registered against this amendment came primarily from small business concerns, which argued that this business practice allowed them to best compete with larger firms. The split between big and small businesses was advantageous to the government. The publicity afforded to this issue made it appear that they were introducing legislation detrimental to and dividing the business community, for the protection of the consumer.[22]

The final report appeared in March, 1952, and dealt exclusively with recommendations aimed at "strengthening and improving ... the procedures, organization and remedies laid down in the Act rather than ... revolutionizing them."[23] The Committee refrained from making any proposals which would substantially change the direction of combines legislation. The central recommendations concerned administration of the Act. The Committee suggested that the functions of the commissioner be separated into two parts in order to eliminate the position's incompatible role of "prosecutor and judge", a change sought by the business interests. Another proposal was for a permanent research division, separate from a special board which would appraise the evidence and issue a report to the minister in charge.[24]

Other recommendations included establishing a close liaison between the proposed board and other government departments whose activities might affect the competitive structure of the economy; combining the relevant sections of the Criminal Code with the Combines Investigation Act; imposing tariff and patent penalties rather than relying solely on monetary fines for those convicted; lifting the statutory limit on fines; making available personnel and monies to investigate monopolistic situations; and setting up a permanent research agency.[25]

The legislation which was eventually enacted omitted many of the Committee's proposals, including the suggestions for a permanent research agency, patent and tariff penalties, the combining of the Criminal Code and Combines Act provisions and the close liaison between various government departments. "These were recommenda-

---

21 *Ibid.*, p. 22.

22 Thorburn, "Pressure Groups in Canadian Politics," p. 159.

23 *Proposals*, p. 18A.

24 The report would include the pertinent evidence, why or why not the organization was operating to the public detriment, and possible solutions.

25 *Proposals*, p. 20A.

tions that would threaten the power positions of large business interests because they involved considering combines as other than isolated
criminal conspiracies."[26]

The legislation did provide for a Director of Investigation and
Research and a Restrictive Trade Practices Commission, thereby splitting the function of the Commissioner in two. The Director could
initiate an investigation, but "the powers needed to pursue an inquiry
effectively ... could only be exercised after authorization by a member
of the Commission."[27] A report would then be sent to the Commission, who in turn would send it to the Minister of Justice. The report
would have to be published within thirty days of its receipt by the
Minister, unless otherwise suggested by the Commission.

The Macquarrie Committee offered no new prohibitions to
strengthen the merger and monopoly aspects of the Act. They did,
however, propose that the Director of Investigation and Research
could carry out an investigation into monopolistic situations or
restraint of trade in relation to any commodity that might be the
subject of trade and commerce. This led to the introduction of a new
section in the Act, Section 42.

The overall direction of the new legislation followed the traditional approach to the regulation and enforcement of combines; that
is, the prosecution and punishment of a small minority of businessmen
who misused their powers.

*According to this view of the combines problem, combines and monopo-
listic practices represent the exceptional activity of a small minority of
businessmen and are shunned by the law-abiding majority.... Dealing
with them is a matter of investigation, criminal prosecution, and punishment by fines. Combines are thus viewed as constituting a police problem
and a legal problem—not an economic problem*[28] *[emphasis added]*.

The Macquarrie Committee, however, attempted to present an overall
report which would deal with the economic realities of a modern
capitalistic system. Their proposals would make the Act much more
effective than simply legal enforcement.[29] However, the new legislation
reflected a compromise not representative of the reality of the situation, since monopolistic practices are normal to businessmen and it

*... serves the purposes of compromise ... since it leads to a policy of
enforcement which provides a few spectacular court cases to which the*

26 Thorburn, "Pressure Groups in Canadian Politics," p. 159.

27 *Proposals*, p. 22A.

28 Rosenbluth and Thorburn, *Canadian Anti-Combines Legislation*, pp. 27-32.

29 Rosenbluth and Thorburn, "Canadian Anti-Combines Legislation," p. 498.

attention of voters can be directed, while leaving most business activity unmolested. Moreover, the high standards of proof required in criminal proceedings lead to an emphasis on documentary evidence, which provides relative immunity to the verbal agreements among a few large firms. Thus, big business is protected. It opposes the Combines Investigation Act but can live with it.[30]

With the defeat of the Liberal party in 1957, the new Conservative government immediately concerned itself with the current nature of combines legislation. During the next two years the government reviewed the legislation allowing various interest groups to make representations to it. The strongest representations were by big business groups, who utilized the powers of prominent lawyers to formulate and present briefs for them. Some of the biggest business interests and associations were well represented, such as the Canadian Pulp and Paper Association, MacMillan Bloedel Limited, the E. B. Eddy Co., as well as the metal mining and electrical manufacturing concerns. Generally, they wished mergers to be held within the public interest, unless a complete monopoly was formed. The government's own proposals "went some distance towards meeting earlier criticisms advanced by businessmen," and so the latter's "comments were directed at obtaining additional concessions and did not go into the matters already conceded by the government."

The bill the government proposed to Parliament in 1959 incorporated many of the suggestions made by big business interests. It was only then that the contents became known to the public, and immediately several consumers', co-operative and agricultural groups began to oppose the bill to protect the existing Act from the weakening amendments. Some of these groups were the Canadian Association of Consumers, the Co-operative Union of Canada, and the Canadian Federation of Agriculture. There were a total of 143 representations on the part of private bodies at this time, of which 100 came from trade associations and business firms.[31] The Minister of Justice withdrew the bill for further study, reintroducing it the next year, after which it was enacted.[32] The Conservatives, in their bill, tried the now familiar compromise of attempting to maintain their image of protecting the public interest, while appeasing large business interests.

The major change in these amendments was that the Criminal Code provision relating to combines was included in the Combines Investigation Act, eliminating the fifty years of duplicity of various

30 *Ibid.*, pp. 498-99.
31 Rosenbluth and Thorburn, *Canadian Anti-Combines Legislation*, p. 89.
32 See Thorburn, "Pressure Groups in Canadian Politics," for a description of the various interest groups involved.

sections. The definition of "combine" was dropped and the word "trust" eliminated, and separate clauses were introduced for mergers and monopolies. Both were now offences "only where they were likely to be, or to operate, to the detriment or against the interest of the public."[33]

Certain provisions were attached to the combine section of the Combines Investigation Act. Rather than the overall prohibition of restraints or competition which are "undue" or "to the detriment of the public," the new act specified that a "conspiracy, combination, agreement, or arrangement" was illegal only if it reduced competition unduly in one of the following: prices, quantity or quality, markets or customers, methods, or entry and expansion of rival firms.[34] The Act thus became "more permissive, making it more difficult to obtain a conviction where agreements with anti-competitive effects exist."[35]

The section dealing with resale price maintenance was weakened, a direct result of big business interests which favoured the deletion of this provision. The "weak link" was a defence clause which allowed the accused to escape conviction if the article was being used for other than a profit, thereby making it almost impossible to secure a conviction.

Summarizing the 1960 amendments, Rosenbluth and Thorburn believe that the " ... wording of the amendments suggests that the rules against agreements and against resale price maintenance have been seriously impaired ... " and " ... the chances of proceeding against mergers have been greatly weakened. . . . "[36]

The administration of the Combines Investigation Act was transferred to the President of the Privy Council from the Minister of Justice in 1965; and to the Registrar General in 1966. In the summer of 1966, the Economic Council of Canada undertook a program to study certain aspects of the Combines Investigation Act "with a view to providing advice as to the course of action that seems best suited to meeting the needs of the Canadian people and the Canadian economy in the consumer field."[37] The whole question of combines, mergers, monopolies, restraint of trade, as well as patents, trade marks, copyrights, etc., was given to the Economic Council to review.

At the end of 1967 the Department of Consumer and Corporate Affairs was established. The first Economic Council of Canada report was published that same year and, from one of the recommendations,

---

33 *Proposals*, p. 23A.
34 Rosenbluth and Thorburn, *Canadian Anti-Combines Legislation*, p. 93.
35 *Ibid.*
36 *Ibid.*, p. 95.
37 *Proposals*, p. 27A.

Section 306, misleading price advertising was transferred to the Combines Investigation Act [Section 33D].

The second report from the Economic Council was the Interim Report on Competition Policy in 1969. Immediately after this report was issued, the Department of Consumer and Corporate Affairs proposed a new bill aimed at saving what D. W. Henry, Director of Research and Investigation, called *"what's left of the free market in Canada"*[38] [italics added]. In the following nine years, the bill was presented to Parliament five times by three different cabinet ministers. When the original minister, Ron Basford, introduced Bill C-256, the new Competition Bill, businessmen sent over 300 briefs to the government showing their concern over the suggested proposals. The business lobby was able to get assurances from the government that it would remove those sections of the bill which might have "unintended effects". "When the bill was sent, in 1971, to the Senate Committee on Banking, Trade, and Commerce for review, 39 of the 40 witnesses who appeared before it were industrial and business groups; the lone dissenter being the Consumers' Association of Canada."[39] The bill was subsequently divided.

This resulted in a two-stage approach to the new bill. The first stage, introduced into Parliament in November, 1973, and enacted January 1, 1976, concerned itself with those measures which received a substantial degree of approval from all sides concerned. This section dealt specifically with business practices such as "double ticketing, pyramid selling, and misleading advertising".[40] The second part was to result from further study of "more contentious matters, namely those of a broader industrial organization nature."[41] This section of the new Competition Act is aimed at such topics as monopolies, mergers, and interlocking directorships.

Stage two of the competition act was announced by the Minister of Consumer and Corporate Affairs, Anthony C. Abbott, on March 16, 1977. Its major proposals included replacing the four-member Restrictive Trade Practices Commission by a Competition Board composed of a maximum of seven permanent and five associate members; the newly created Board could allow corporate mergers and monopolistic practices if they were judged more efficient, particularly for international competition; criminal penalties would be removed for merger violators; class action suits would be allowed within certain guidelines.[42] Most

38 *Ibid.*, pp. 29A-31A.
39 Mitchell, *The Politics of Food*, p. 193.
40 *Ibid.*
41 *Ibid.*
42 *Proposals for a New Competition Policy for Canada: Second Stage* (Ottawa: Minister of Supply and Services Canada; 1977).

public attention to the new legislation has focused upon the positive sanctioning of monopolisitic practices. This aspect of the legislation represents a dramatic shift in philosophy. Rather than viewing monopolies in private industry as inherently suspect and contrary to the public interest, they are viewed as potentially positive. Particular emphasis by the government was placed upon Canada's lack of real international competitiveness in the marketplace. Thus, an independent and strong Canadian economy in relation to the world market is envisioned through such policies. It is interesting to note that such an appeal is being made, notwithstanding the effect of such monopolies upon home markets. As Minister Abbott stated:

"As long as companies can show that they will be more efficient by merging or by acting as monopolies, even if competition in home markets suffers, then they should be allowed to do so."[43]

While the government recognizes that attempts to prosecute mergers for their potential monopolistic effects has been a colossal failure, rather than attempting to change the law to make such prosecutions more obtainable, the opposite approach is taken. The specifics of these and other aspects of the proposed legislation will be more fully discussed in Chapter 7.

Whatever the outcome of the current study and proposals of Part II of the new Competition Bill, this historical account of Canadian anti-combines legislation has shown that the federal government has not lived up to the philosophy behind combines legislation. The government may never realistically eliminate all restraint of trade practices and economic concentration in Canada, but an examination of the intentions of governments since 1889 may indicate that their public statements and their undeclared intentions were at opposite ends of the pole. Illegal trade practices have generally proceeded unhindered, despite numerous committee reports which point to serious deficiencies in our system of "free and open enterprise". While each member of parliament may personally dislike combines legislation, or simply represent corporate disapproval in their constituency, the two major parties in Canada have attempted to render the legislation ineffective through their varying economic philosophies, all of which have a traditional[44] viewpoint about regulating the business sector. Indeed, one of the most serious deficiencies of combines legislation is that regulation is left in the hands of the judiciary. Simply relying on legal reasoning, devoid of an economic interpretation of the alleged viola-

---

43 "New Reform Bills Allow Monopoly if Found Efficient," *The Calgary Herald* (March 17, 1977), p. 1.

44 Thorburn, "Pressure Groups in Canadian Politics," p. 157.

tion's impact upon the economy, is not necessarily to the best advantage of the public interest, as the judiciary convicts only those mergers which have eliminated all competition in an area once considered to be competitive.

The federal government has attempted to publicly present itself as the protector of the free enterprise system in the name of the public interest through striking parliamentary committees, royal commissions, and other government appointed bodies. But the lack of relevant measures to maintain competition in the Canadian economy can be seen as the outcome of a long-standing and almost traditional belief held by King and those who followed him that large corporations which control a great portion of the market are basically beneficial to the needs and life chances of the Canadian public. Canadian combines legislation has been the result of the government's close relationships with the business sector. The connections between these two groups have been documented in Canadian social science literature.[45] These links have also been found on government boards of inquiry and committees with instructions to investigate alleged illegal activities by business concerns. Members of these government bodies usually have a close connection with those they are investigating, a situation which ultimately makes the committee ineffective.

The connections between government and private industry need not be intimate, although to a considerable degree they are. It is sufficient that they accept as the basis of a common working relationship the assumption of 'non-intervention' by the state in the market determinations of a private economy. From that basis of understanding, the gamesmanship of protecting the public interest can be tolerated by business whatever its nuisance implications. Businessmen know that without the credibility of 'public watch-dog' earned for government by the rhetoric of the Herb Grays, Beryl Plumptres and André Ouellets things could be much worse. The issue of inflation might be drawn more clearly along class lines, with *consequences frightening for the average business executive to contemplate.*[46]

The Royal Commission on Corporate Concentration in Canada (or Bryce Commission) is an example of this close relationship between government and industry. It was formed as a result of Power Corporation's (Montreal Trust, Great-West Life, Imperial Life Assurance Co. of Canada, Consolidated Bathurst Ltd., etc.) attempt to acquire control of the Argus Corporation (Standard Broadcasting Corp., Dominion Stores, Domtar, Massey-Ferguson, B.C. Forest Prod-

---

45 See for example, Clement, *The Canadian Elite.*

46 Mitchell, *The Politics of Food*, pp. 194-95.

ucts Ltd., etc.), a move which would lead to one huge corporation controlling many areas of the Canadian economy, as well as the solidification of strong connections with the Liberal and Conservative parties at the provincial and federal levels.[47] The three-man committee was chaired by Robert Bryce, the Deputy Minister of Finance from 1963 to 1970, and "it is not altogether probable that he will be prepared to give a harsh assessment of the mass of economic regulations he had an intimate part in shaping. . . . "[48] The other members included Robert Dickerson, a tax specialist with a corporate law firm in Vancouver, and Pierre Nadeau, president of Petrofina Canada and a director of the Royal Bank. It is interesting to note that the Royal Bank offered a $70 million loan to Power Corp. to take over Argus Corp., and it is possible that a "conflict of interest arises, since a director of the Royal would have an interest in seeing the deal go through."[49]

During the first part of the hearings held by the Bryce Commission, fifty-one briefs were presented with thirty-five representing business interests. The three commissioners were friendly with witnesses from the corporate community but remained aloof from the anti-corporate witnesses. The lack of an opposing viewpoint on the Commission seems to be more than an oversight on the part of the Liberal government. It seems to suggest that the government's motivation and ability to investigate, let alone regulate, the business community in Canada is questionable. Public disapproval and demands for the regulation of these matters may have led to some government action, but it has been weak, superficial and ineffective in getting to the crux of the issues. Indeed, the enacted combines laws have seemed to "inflict minimum inconvenience on business, consistent with the government's need to convince ordinary citizens that it is against monopoly."[50] The government in power has been able to deflect public protest while appearing to do something about the problem, thereby avoiding the real issue which stands before them. As Bert Young has summarized, the government has not been concerned with the growth and impact of corporations on the Canadian economy, and, "if anything, they have encouraged it."[51]

---

47 Cy Gonick, *Inflation or Depression* (Toronto: James Lorimer and Company, 1975), pp. 32-36.

48 Eric Hamovitch, "The Bryce Probe Probed," *The Last Post 5* (June, 1976), p. 36.

49 *Ibid.*, p. 37.

50 I. Drummond, *The Canadian Economy: Structure and Development*, rev. ed. (Georgetown: Irwin Dorsey, 1972), p. 101.

51 Bert Young, "Corporate Interests and the State," *Our Generation* 10, No. 1 (Winter-Spring, 1974), p. 77.

CHAPTER 6

Criminal Corporations: The Official Record

Unlike the criminals of the underworld, the permissive criminals of the upperworld have never been marked off and dramatized as a distinct group upon which public disapproval could be focused. They have never been rounded up by the police nor gathered together in a prison where they could be examined, cursed into some semblance of uniformity, and talked about as a special type of human being. Instead, they have been scattered among us as friends and fellow members in clubs and churches. They have contributed to organizations for the treatment of juvenile delinquents and have served in legislatures passing laws to check crime.

Albert Morris, *Criminology* (New York: Longmans Green, 1935), p. 152.

Introduction

The main objective of this chapter is to identify the major Canadian
corporations which have violated the Combines Act and have subsequently been investigated by the Combines Branch. The reports of
1952 to 1973 prepared by the Director of Investigation and the
Restrictive Trade Practices Commission, as well as the decisions
handed down by the Attorney General of Canada, have been
researched in order to compile the data relating specifically to the
quantity and types of illegal actions precipitated by the largest manufacturing, mining, and merchandising corporations in Canada.[1] The
names of the largest corporations have been taken from lists supplied
by the *Financial Post* and, more recently, the monthly journal *Canadian Business*. These lists are used to identify the largest corporations
on a year-to-year basis. Sutherland's[2] procedure of selecting the top
United States corporations from lists totalled over a ten-year time span
is inappropriate for our use because many Canadian corporations have
merged with others since 1952, and will subsequently not be included
in a summary of activity in a ten-year period except perhaps as a
corporation with a minor standing.

Not all of Sutherland's methods will be changed. This study will
follow his technique of applying the decisions of the various individuals and commissions concerning subsidiaries of corporations to their
controlling, or parent, companies for the period during which the
parent corporations have been in their positions of control. Likewise,
any decision concerning one of the corporations is considered to be
the unit of tabulation.[3] This means that if a decision is made concerning four corporations, it is counted four times, once for each corporation in question. Similarly, if two separate decisions are made concerning a single corporation in a single case, then each is counted. However, if one decision includes several counts—this is especially true in
misleading price advertising decisions—then the decision is counted
only once. Our analysis of the criminality of Canadian corporations
concerns itself with the following types of acts: combinations, mergers,
monopolies, resale price maintenance, misleading price advertising,
predatory pricing, price discrimination, and violations of patents.

1 This twenty-one-year period was selected because of the new Combines Act
   introduced that year and because a consistent list of Canada's top corporations
   began in 1951.

2 Edwin H. Sutherland, *White Collar Crime* (New York: Holt, Rinehart and
   Winston, 1949).

3 The term "decisions" is utilized according to Sutherland's usage in *White Collar
   Crime*, pp. 19-20, which includes "not only the formal decisions of administrative
   commissions, stipulations accepted by the court or commission, settlements ordered
   or approved by the court ...."

The Corporate Criminal Record

Some of the largest Canadian corporations, identified on a year-to-year basis, have committed acts violating the combines laws and decisions determining their acts to be offences under the Combines Act have been handed down. Table 6-1 summarizes the total number of decisions made against Canada's largest corporations, by year, 1952 to 1972. A total number of 157 decisions have been made against the fifty largest corporations over the twenty-one-year period. The greatest number of decisions have been made against combinations (ninety-five, or 60% of the total), misleading price advertising (twenty-four, or 15.2%), and mergers (twenty, or 12.7%), with the remaining five types of violations accounting for the other nineteen (or 12.1%) decisions made against the largest corporations. On a year-to-year basis, not taking into account recidivism of the large corporations, for the twenty-one-year span under investigation, an average of 2.4 decisions has been rendered against the largest corporations, in comparison with an average of 29.1 decisions for all other companies and corporations in the same time span (see Table 6-2). During this twenty-one-year period the Combines Branch failed to reach a decision against a large corporation in four years (1957, 1959, 1963 and 1968), while, for another nine years, the total number of decisions against large corporations failed to exceed 10% of the total number of decisions (1954, 1960, 1964, 1965, 1967, 1969, 1970, 1971, and 1972). The year the greatest number of decisions were recorded against the top corporations was 1962, when fifteen of the twenty-five decisions (60%) dealt with the largest corporations.

If this twenty-one-year period were to be divided into three equal seven-year periods (Table 6-3), it can be noted that both the total number and percentage of the decisions concerned with large corporations have steadily decreased since the first seven-year period of 1952-1958. The last period, 1966 to 1972, illustrates that while the total number of decisions increased by 146 (or 47.9%) from the previous period, the total number of actual decisions registered against the largest corporations decreased by four, leading to a reduction of over 60% with regard to the decisions concerning the largest corporations.

Over half (58%) of the largest corporations have been recidivists (see Table 6-1). The fifty largest corporations have had an average of 3.2 decisions registered against them, ranging from a low of one to a high of twenty-three decisions. Only three corporations have had ten or more decisions handed down against them; two of them (Domtar Limited and Canadian International Paper Company) are in the lumber/pulp and paper industry, which accounts for 20.9% of the total decisions against the largest corporations. The industries in which the

TABLE 6-1.   DECISIONS AGAINST CANADA'S LARGEST CORPORATIONS, 1952-1972

Name of Corporation	Combine	Merger	Monopoly	Price Discrimination	Predatory Pricing	Resale Price Maintenance	Patents	Misleading Price Advertising	TOTAL
Domtar Limited	19	4	—	—	—	—	—	—	23
George Weston Limited	9	—	—	—	—	—	—	3	12
Canadian International Paper Company	7	3	—	—	—	—	—	—	10
Warnock Hersey International Ltd.	4	4	—	—	—	—	—	—	8
Crown Zellerbach Limited	4	2	—	—	—	—	—	—	6
Shell Canada Limited	1	1	1	—	—	2	—	1	6
Simpsons-Sears Limited	—	—	—	—	—	—	—	6	6
Hudson's Bay Mining & Smelting Co.	1	1	1	1	1	—	—	—	5
Continental Can Co. of Canada	3	1	—	—	—	—	—	—	4
Dominion Foundry & Steel Corp.	4	—	—	—	—	—	—	—	4
T. Eaton Company	—	—	—	—	—	—	—	4	4
Safeway, Incorporated	2	—	—	—	—	1	—	1	4
Abitibi Paper Company	3	—	—	—	—	—	—	—	3
Anthes Imperial Limited	—	1	1	—	1	—	—	—	3
Canada Cement Lafarge Limited	3	—	—	—	—	—	—	—	3
Canadian General Electric	1	—	1	—	—	1	—	—	3
Consolidated Paper Company	3	—	—	—	—	—	—	—	3
Dominion Bridge Company	3	—	—	—	—	—	—	—	3
Emco Limited	3	—	—	—	—	—	—	—	3
Steel Company of Canada Limited	3	—	—	—	—	—	—	—	3
Union Carbide Corporation	1	—	—	—	—	—	2	—	3
Westinghouse Canada Limited	1	—	1	—	—	1	—	—	3
Canada Packers Limited	1	1	—	—	—	—	—	—	2

TABLE 6-1   (cont'd.)

Gulf Oil Canada Limited	–	–	–	1	–	1	–	–	2
Hawker Siddeley Canada Limited	2	–	–	–	–	–	–	–	2
Imasco Limited	1	–	–	–	–	–	–	1	2
MacMillan Bloedel Limited	1	1	–	–	–	–	–	–	2
Southam Publishing Company	1	1	–	–	–	–	–	–	2
Standard Oil Co. of B.C. Limited	1	–	–	–	–	–	–	1	2
Atlantic Sugar Refineries Limited	1	–	–	–	–	–	–	–	1
Bell Canada	1	–	–	–	–	–	–	–	1
Burns Foods Limited	1	–	–	–	–	–	–	–	1
Canadian Breweries Limited	1	–	–	–	–	–	–	–	1
Canadian Industries Limited	–	–	1	–	–	–	–	–	1
Canadian Johns-Manville Company	1	–	–	–	–	–	–	–	1
Canadian Tire Corporation	–	–	–	–	–	–	–	1	1
Dominion Stores Limited	–	–	–	–	–	–	–	1	1
Federal Grain Company	1	–	–	–	–	–	–	–	1
General Foods	–	–	–	–	–	–	–	1	1
B. F. Goodrich Canada Limited	1	–	–	–	–	–	–	–	1
Goodyear Tire & Rubber Co. of Canada	1	–	–	–	–	–	–	–	1
Hudson's Bay Company	–	–	–	–	–	–	–	1	1
S. S. Kresge Company	–	–	–	–	–	–	–	1	1
M. Loeb Limited	–	–	–	–	–	–	–	1	1
McLaren Power & Paper Company	1	–	–	–	–	–	–	–	1
Molson Industries Limited	–	–	–	–	–	–	–	1	1
The Price Company Limited	1	–	–	–	–	–	–	–	1
Reed Paper Group	1	–	–	–	–	–	–	–	1
Sogmeines Limited	1	–	–	–	–	–	–	–	1
Texaco Canada Limited	–	–	–	1	–	–	–	–	1
TOTALS	95	20	6	3	2	6	2	23	157

SOURCE: Skeoch, 1966a; Restrictive Trade Practices Commission Reports 1952-1962; Canada, 1973

TABLE 6-2.   DECISIONS AGAINST TOTAL NUMBER OF COMPANIES AND
CORPORATIONS, AND LARGEST CORPORATIONS, BY YEAR,
1952-1972

Year	Total Number of All Decisions against Corporations by Year	Total Number of Decisions against Large Corporations by Year	Per Cent of Decisions against Large Corporations
1952	48	14	29.2
1953	29[a]	4	13.7
1954	57[b]	3	5.3
1955	25	6	24.0
1956	47	10	21.3
1957	7	0	0.0
1958	21	9	42.9
1959	12[c]	0	0.0
1960	36	3	8.3
1961	4	1	25.0
1962	25	15	60.0
1963	5	0	0.0
1964	59	3	5.0
1965	18	1	5.6
1966	55[d]	8	14.5
1967	12	1	8.3
1968	23[e]	0	0.0
1969	74	3	3.1
1970	66[f]	3	4.6
1971	36[g]	1	2.8
1972	39	3	7.7
TOTAL[h]	698	88[i]	11.2

SOURCE: Skeoch, 1966a; Restrictive Trade Practices Commission Reports 1952-1962;
Canada, 1973

[a] This total includes decisions against 1 individual and 2 associations.
[b] This total includes decision against 1 association.
[c] This total includes decisions against 5 individuals and 3 associations.
[d] This total includes decisions against 13 individuals and 3 associations.
[e] This total includes decisions against 14 individuals and 1 association.
[f] This total includes decisions against 1 association.
[g] This total includes decisions against 6 individuals and 2 associations.
[h] These totals do not include misleading advertising decisions, which are in Table 6-4.
[i] The total number of decisions against large corporations in Tables 6-1 and 6-2 differ,
due to, in part, that the total in Table 6-2 does not include decisions regarding
misleading price advertising (see Table 6-4). In addition, the total in Table 6-1
includes decisions against the subsidiaries of large corporations, whereas in Table 6-2
they are not included, which accounts for the remaining differences in the totals. (i.e.,
in Table 6-1, one large corporation and 3 of its subsidiaries would count as 4
decisions, whereas in Table 6-2 this would only count as one.)

TABLE 6-3. DECISIONS AGAINST ALL COMPANIES AND CORPORATIONS
AND LARGEST CORPORATIONS BY SEVEN-YEAR PERIODS

	Decisions against All Companies, Corporations, Associations, and Individuals	*Decisions against Largest Corporations*	*Percentage of Decisions against Largest Corporations*
1952-1958	234	46	19.7
1959-1965	159	23	14.5
1966-1972	305	19	5.1

greatest amount of official criminality is found are the lumber/pulp
and paper industry and the steel industry, accounting for approximately 40% of all decisions among the large corporations.

Table 6-4, a separate enumeration of misleading price advertising
violations, shows that of the 282 decisions concerning companies and
corporations under this section of the Combines Act, only twenty-four,
or 8.5% have been directed toward the largest corporations. Twenty-
one of these decisions were made in 1971 and 1972. Of these twenty-
four decisions, six (25%) have been made against Simpsons-Sears
Limited, four (16.7%) against the T. Eaton Company, and three
(12.5%) against George Weston Limited. Thus, thirteen (54.2%) of the
decisions concerning misleading price advertising among the largest
corporations have been made against only three of the largest Canadian corporations.

TABLE 6-4. MISLEADING PRICE ADVERTISING DECISIONS, BY YEAR,
1952-1972

Year	*Total No. of Decisions against All Corporations*	*Total No. of Decisions against Largest Corporations*	*Percent of Decisions against Largest Corporations*
1962	6	0	0.0
1963	6	0	0.0
1964	2	0	0.0
1965	5	0	0.0
1966	6	1	16.7
1967	5	0	0.0
1968	16	1	6.4
1969	22	0	0.0
1970	45	1	2.2
1971	80	9	10.1
1972	89	12	13.4
TOTALS	282	24	8.5

Intercorporate Crime

Only rarely does the Combines Investigation Branch investigate an alleged restraint of trade agreement involving more than one or two large corporations. On most occasions, it is happy to direct its efforts toward less prestigious victims. Indeed, the last investigation into several large Canadian corporations at one time occurred in 1966, when an alleged combination for the distribution and sale of mandarin oranges was investigated by the Attorney General of Canada. This lack of investigation does not preclude the involvement of several large Canadian corporations directly—or indirectly—in a combines case through joint ownership of various companies.

Prior to this last case in 1966, however, the Combines Branch occasionally investigated certain illegal agreements extending through many large Canadian corporations. The combines case we use as an example of intercorporate crime was originally investigated during 1958 by the Restrictive Trade Practices Commission, and concerned an alleged combination in the supply of pulpwood throughout Eastern Canada. The Director decided to prosecute the companies and corporations involved upon the receipt of the Commission's report, and was successful in obtaining convictions against a total of seventeen companies and corporations. Table 6-5 outlines the penalties, totalling $250 000, imposed upon each of the accused.

TABLE 6-5.   VARIOUS AMOUNTS OF IMPOSED PENALTIES IN PULPWOOD CASE

Company or Corporation Charged	Penalty
Canadian International Paper Company	$25 000
Howard Smith Paper Mills Limited	25 000
St. Lawrence Corporation Limited	20 000
The E. B. Eddy Company	20 000
Anglo-Canadian Pulp and Paper Mills Limited	20 000
Consolidated Paper Corporation Limited	20 000
Abitibi Power and Paper Company Limited	15 000
Gaspesia Sulphite Company Limited	15 000
St.-Anne Power Company	10 000
The Ontario Paper Company Limited	10 000
Donnacona Paper Limited	10 000
The KVP Company Limited	10 000
Richmond Pulp and Paper Company of Canada Limited	8 000
The James McLaren Company Limited	8 000
Armstrong Forest Company	8 000
Gair Company of Canada Limited	8 000
Spruce Falls Pulp and Paper Company Limited	8 000

This one case involved two corporations (Canadian International Paper Company and the Consolidated Paper Corporation Limited) and fifteen companies, thirteen of which were subsidiaries of eleven corporations identified in Table 6-6. An investigation of the intercorporate holdings of the 13 corporations involved in this case reveals that they are interwoven through joint ownership of various companies (not necessarily those convicted). This fact dispels the notion that these corporations may have joined together for a "one-shot" agreement to practice restraint of trade. The investigation also exposed the fact that other pulp and paper corporations were closely related to those involved, specifically the Reed Paper Group, Crown Zellerbach (Canada) Limited, MacMillan Bloedel Limited, Brown Forest Industries Limited, and the New York Times Company. Thus many major Canadian lumber and pulp-and-paper corporations are joined together and can effectively control a large degree of the Canadian market. These corporations are also indirectly related to other major Canadian corporations: for instance, Domtar Limited controlled 17.5% of Junior-Frood Mines, which was also controlled by the Canadian Imperial Bank of Commerce (13.4%), and Falconbridge Nickel National Trust Company (18.2%). Also, the Kimberly-Clark Corporation controlled 35% of the Irving Pulp and Paper Company, with the remainder being owned by the K. C. Irving Company which controlled thirty-three companies, and was related through two companies to Standard Oil Company (B.C.) Limited.

Relating specifically to the pulpwood case in question, the Canadian Overseas Paper Company was jointly owned by seven different corporations, with control being either at 14.1% or 14.3%. MacMillan Bloedel Limited and Canadian International Paper Company each controlled 14.1%, and Consolidated Paper Corporation, Domtar Limited, Associated Newspapers Limited, Abitibi Paper Company Limited, and Crown Zellerbach (Canada) Limited controlled 14.3% each. In addition, Consolidated Paper Corporation and Canadian International Paper Company linked the other five corporations which owned Canadian Overseas Paper Company indirectly to George Weston Limited, a major food empire, because those 2 corporations and George Weston were joint owners of the Upper Ottawa Improvement Company. Similarly, all the above-mentioned corporations were indirectly linked, through Domtar Limited, and Associated Newspapers Limited to the Reed Paper Group and the American Can Corporation, as all four jointly controlled Ormiston Mining and Smelting Company Limited. Thus, as Figure 6-1 illustrates, all of the corporations mentioned in Table 6-6—except the Tribune Company and the McLaren Power and Paper Company—and other significant pulp and paper organizations are directly or indirectly related through only seven companies!

Thus, this chart illustrates how large Canadian corporations are

TABLE 6-6.   INVESTIGATED CORPORATIONS AND THEIR SUBSIDIARIES

Name of Corporation	Subsidiary Convicted
Abitibi Paper Company Limited	Abitibi Power and Paper Company Ltd.
Abitibi Paper Company Limited	St.-Anne Power Company
Associated Newspapers Limited	Gaspesia Sulphite Company Limited
Domtar Limited	St. Lawrence Corporation Limited
Domtar Limited	Howard Smith Mills Limited
George Weston Limited	The E. B. Eddy Company
Tribune Company	Ontario Paper Company Limited
Kimberly-Clark Corporation	Spruce Falls Pulp & Paper Company Ltd.
Continental Can Company Inc.	Gair Company of Canada Limited
McLaren Power & Paper Company	The James McLaren Company Limited
KVP Sutherland Company	The KVP Company Limited
Kruger Organization Limited	Richmond Pulp & Paper Co. of Canada Ltd.
American Can Corporation Limited	Anglo-American Pulp & Paper Mills Ltd.

directly and indirectly related to each other, providing many routes of access in order to achieve restraint of trade agreements and to control the markets in a broad area of products.

Conclusion

The data researched and collected in this chapter suggest that the Combines Branch has centred its attentions upon the investigation, prosecution, and conviction of small- and medium-sized companies and corporations, leaving the very largest corporations free to engage in their monopolistic practices. Rosenbluth, in his research of the Combines Investigation Branch in the early 1960s, found an inverse correlation between the effectiveness of this government branch and the size of the firms investigated, prosecuted, and successfully convicted, the largest corporations enjoying a criminal-free record even though they engaged in much criminal activity.

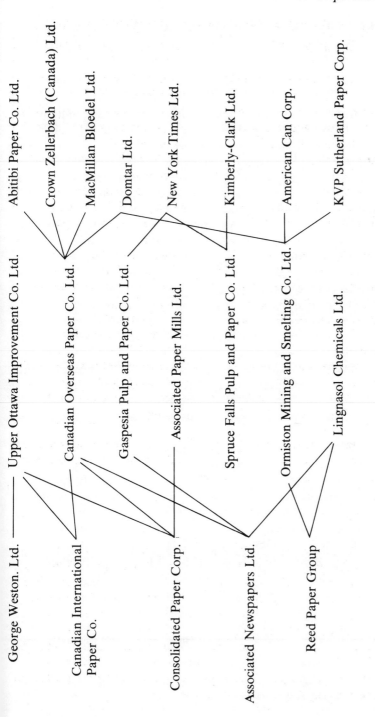

FIGURE 6-1.   INTERCORPORATE RELATIONS OF THIRTEEN CANADIAN
CORPORATIONS RELATED TO THE PULPWOOD CASE

Investigation and prosecutions are aimed primarily at local markets and small firms. More specifically, ... the size of firms investigated with successful (conviction) was small, firms investigated but with no action taken somewhat larger, and firms of high concentration with national markets ... have generally avoided investigation altogether.[4]

While of course some of the largest Canadian corporations are investigated each year, our data suggest that the actual number of mergers investigated has decreased to the point of non-existence. And when the number of mergers each year and the current degree of concentration are compared to the largest corporations investigated each year, an inverse relationship appears between them. Thus, while potentially illegal restraint of trade agreements and monopolistic situations are increasing, those corporations which are involved in such situations are benefitting from the protection afforded by the government's legislation and the lack of enforcement on the part of the Combines Branch. As Mitchell puts it, two possible conclusions arise from this lack of regulation of the largest corporations: "One is that small businessmen are more 'crooked' than the nation's corporate elite. The other, more obvious answer ... is that the Anti-Combines Administration is neither able, nor willing, nor intended to influence the real forces which run the economy."[5]

This does not mean that the personnel of the Combines Branch are not adept in their positions. Nor does it mean that all the Directors have been "confidants" to the interests of big business. Rather, as Rosenbluth and Thorburn suggest, this ineffective administration of the Combines Investigation Act is the result of a compromise on the part of the federal government to satisfy both the public *and* big business.[6] Discussing the "cops-and-robbers" concept of the Combines Branch, they point out that combines officers are highly specialized and trained in legalistic matters, with research economists considered to be mere "frills". Moreover, the emphasis is placed upon successful convictions; prosecutions are only pursued in such cases where the law is clear and the companies involved in an illegal activity are clearly violating the Combines Act. "The practice of turning prosecutions over to lawyers in private practice has emphasized the legalistic bias, which

4 Don Mitchell, *The Politics of Food* (Toronto: James Lorimer and Company, 1975), p. 175.

5 *Ibid.*

6 G. Rosenbluth and H. Thorburn, *Canadian Anti-Combines Legislation 1952-1960* (Toronto: University of Toronto Press, 1963).

avoids cases involving monopoly, merger and price discrimination, where economic analysis is essential."[7]

Evidence is not easy to secure, especially among large corporations which can work through a legitimate company owned by the majority of them, making written agreements between them unnecessary. However, smaller firms which are involved in restraint of trade practices are more likely to be involved with a greater number of firms and thus some written records may possibly exist. Mitchell comments that the way mergers and combines are treated as a legalistic, policing problem rather than in the context of their economic realities in the modern capitalistic system, "is artificial to the point of being absurd."[8]

It appears the government's legislation and enforcement concerning combines is not directed to prosecuting the greatest violators, i.e., the largest business corporations but, rather, is a response to the interests of such organizations, leading to a "pathetic and revealing commentary on government-industry collusion."[9] No longer can we afford to believe that the government maintains a neutral stance. Rather than the various interest groups of society competing on equal grounds from various platforms, one group has emerged whose requirements are looked after first. "It would seem, then, that the Canadian social structure, rather than having a plurality of power centres, is dominated by a concentration of oligopolies which, to a considerable degree, control the economic life of the country."[10]

---

7 *Ibid.*, p. 103.

8 Mitchell, *The Politics of Food*, p. 176.

9 *Ibid.*

10 Bert Young, "Corporate Interests and the State, *Our Generation*, 10 (Winter-Spring, 1975), p. 81.

CHAPTER 7

The Government's Record: Enforcement of Combines Laws

It is better, so the image runs, to take one dime from each of ten million people at the point of a corporation than $100,000 from each of ten banks at the point of a gun. It is also safer.

C. Wright Mills, *The Power Elite* (New York: Oxford University Press, 1956), p. 95.

This chapter empirically tests the Canadian government's role as a neutral agency and upholder of the "competitive market" through the enforcement of combines laws. To evaluate the government's "record" in this area, this section is composed of three parts: the actual enforcement record of combines laws by the federal government, 1889-1972; the number of mergers and the prosecution of them by the government as well as the degree of economic concentration in various industrial sectors; and the amount of financial assistance and the number of employees allowed to the Combines Branch by the federal government.

Enforcement Record

Table 7-1 summarizes the record of enforcement in combines cases by the Canadian government according to the various combines acts, 1889-1972. Of the 158 reports actually undertaken and completed by the various boards, directors, and other administrative bodies charged with enforcing the combines laws since 1910, a total of 136 were published. The government receives its information concerning alleged illegal business activity from various sources, e.g., the public, other government departments, etc. On some basis, which is not revealed in the Annual Reports of the Combines Investigation Act, the Director of Restrictive Trade Practices Commission decides to open an investigation into certain alleged violations and, at the conclusion of such an investigation, a report is issued, from which it is established whether or not to press charges. These reports must be published, as specified by the Combines Act since 1910. Until recently, however, the government has oftentimes refused to issue a report; this refusal was greatest while the 1923 to 1939 legislation was in effect, and especially when the Conservatives were in power. Then twelve of the twenty-six reports (or 46%) remained unpublished. Prosecution procedures are not usually started unless there is an excellent chance of conviction based upon legal criteria[1] and, from all the reports published since 1910, the government has secured eighty-four (62%) convictions, fourteen acquittals, thirty-eight "no action" taken, and three cases in which the verdict is still to be decided. Tables 7-2 through 7-5 deal with the reports undertaken by the Combines Branch according to the various acts, 1923 through 1972, excluding actions taken under the misleading advertising section of the Combines Investigation Act enacted in 1960.

---

1 Gideon Rosenbluth and Henry Thorburn, *Canadian Anti-Combines Legislation 1952-1960* (Toronto: University of Toronto Press, 1963), p. 103.

No individual has ever been jailed for illegal activities under the Combines Act.[2] Cases concerning misleading advertising are summarized in Table 7-6, which illustrates that 83% of the cases under this section of the Combines Act[3] have been convicted.

Table 7-7 indicates the expanse of the operations of the Bureau of Competition Policy excluding misleading advertising cases, 1954-55 to 1971-72. In this table it can be noted that while the number of *complaints* over the specified eighteen-year period have totalled 2545 for all sections of the Combines Act, for the same eighteen-year time period over 4400 mergers have taken place (Table 7-8), all of which may violate one section of the Combines Act. In addition, the total number of formal inquiries in progress between the years 1954-55 and 1971-72 was 827, a minimal effort on the part of the government to regulate possible illegal activities. As well, only four research projects were completed in the eight years from 1964-65 to 1971-72. These reports are a necessary function of the Branch, providing investigation of various sectors of the economy for possible violations under the Combines Investigation Act.

Mergers and Concentration

Concentration in the various industrial sectors of the Canadian economy is often the result of mergers, and these are within the regulation of the Combines Act. The concern over mergers and concentration in business shown by those in charge of regulating the Act is invaluable for examining the nature and extent of the federal government's intentions about enforcing anti-combines legislation.[4] The level of concentration—the extent to which a small number of firms account for the bulk of an industry's output—has an important effect upon the degree of competitiveness in the economy. This level of concentration is thus subject to the criteria of the Combines Act as those involved may take advantage of their market power to control a particular industry nationally, regionally, or locally.[5] Mitchell points out that the

2 Bruce C. McDonald, "Criminality and the Canadian Anti-Combines Laws," *Alberta Law Review*, 9, No. I (1965), p. 77.

3 Action prior to 1952 is not included, due to the emphasis of the government upon associations of small manufacturers, wholesalers, and retailers, and the lack of information available concerning the size of corporations for the years previous to this date.

4 The number of mergers can be found in the Annual Reports of the Director of Investigation, Combines Branch. It is one of the few areas which affords the public an overall picture of the regulation of Canadian Combines Legislation, as yearly totals are readily accessible to the public.

5 Max Stewart, *Concentration in Canadian Manufacturing and Mining Industries* (Ottawa: Information Canada, 1970), p. 79.

TABLE 7-1. THE CANADIAN GOVERNMENTS ENFORCEMENT OF THE
COMBINES INVESTIGATION ACT 1889-1972

Year	Number of Reports		Decisions	
	Completed	Published		
1889-1900	1		1	acquitted
1900-1910	5		1	acquitted
			4	convicted
1910-1922	1		1	"no action" taken [charged but not constrained]
1923-1939[a]	26	14[f]	4	acquitted
			6	convicted
			7	"no action" taken
1940-1949[b]	9	6	3	convicted
			1	acquitted
			2	"no action" taken
1950-1959[c]	31	31	18	convicted (5 of which were settled out of court)
			3	acquittals
			10	"no action" taken
1960-1972[d]	85	48[e]	57	convicted
			6	acquittals
			19	"no action" taken
			3	no decision reached

[a] See Table 7-2 concerning government combines activity 1923-1939 legislation
[b] See Table 7-3 concerning government combines activity 1940-1949 legislation
[c] See Table 7-4 concerning government combines activity 1950-1959 legislation
[d] See Table 7-5 concerning government combines activity 1960-1972 legislation
[e] The remaining 37 cases were referred directly to the Attorney General of Canada
pursuant to Section 15 of the Combines Investigation Act (1960). No report need be
published. However, for the convenience of assessing the total number of reports
published, these were counted as published as the results are readily available to the
public. One report was not published in 1962 (See Table 7-5).
[f] During the years 1931-32 three reports were not published even though [1] a combine
was found to exist in the flour milling industry [see Skeoch, 1966a]; [2] a combine was
found to exist between radio tube manufacturers [Skeoch, 1966a. p. 104]; [3] a
combine within the Canadian Fruit Basket Pool was convicted [see Skeoch, 1966a, p.
104].

SOURCES:L. Skeoch, *Restrictive Trade Practices in Canada,* Toronto:
McClelland and Stewart, 1966; B. Young, "Corporate Interests and the State",
Our Generation 10 (Winter-Spring, 1974) pp. 70-83; Canada, *Proposal for a
New Competitive Policy for Canada* (Ottawa: Queens Printer, 1973).

TABLE 7-2.   GOVERNMENT COMBINES ACTIVITY 1923-1939 LEGISLATION

Year	Charge	Industry	Report Published	Convicted	Acquitted	No Action	Penalty
1925	combine	fruits and vegetables	*	*			Individuals fined $25,000
1925	combine	coal	*		*		and jailed for
1925	combine	potatoes	*			*	one day;
1926	combine	bread	*			*	corporations
1926	combine	fruits and vegetables	*			*	fined $25,000[a]
1927	combine	druggists	*			*	
1929	combine	milk				*	
1929	combine	matches				*	
1929	combine	plumbing and heating	*	*			Fines totalling $18,700
1930	combine	electrical	*	*			Fines totalling $25,000
1931	combine	bread-baking				*	
1931	combine	motion-pictures	*		*		
1931	combine	flour-milling				*	
1931	combine	radio tubes				*	
1932	combine	fruit baskets		*			Fines totalling $1,500
1933	combine	tobacco	*			*	
1933	combine	coal	*	*			Fines totalling $43,500
1934	combine	footwear				*	
1934	combine	gasoline				*	
1937	monopoly	clay products				*	
1938	combine	fruits and vegetables				*	

Year	Charge	Industry	Report Published	Convicted	Acquitted	No Action	Penalty
1938	combine	tobacco	*		*		
1939	combine	paperboard	*	*			Fines totalling $178,500
1939	combine	gasoline				*	
1939	combine	fruits and vegetables	*		*		
1939	combine	wood preservation				*	

a These fines covered all the offences, not only those under the Combines Investigation Act. The one-day jail term was on separate charges not pertaining to combines (Skeoch, 1966a:97).
SOURCE: Skeoch, 1966a.

TABLE 7-3   GOVERNMENT COMBINES ACTIVITY 1940-1949 LEGISLATION

Year	*Charge*	*Industry*	*Report Published*	Decision			*Penalty*
				Convicted	*Acquitted*	*No Action*	
1946	combine	ammunition				*	
1947	combine	dental supplies	*		*		
1948	combine based on patents	optical goods	*			*	Association disbanded
1948	combine	bread-baking	*	*			Fines totalling $30,000
1948	combine	flour-milling	*		*		
1949	combine	gasoline			*		
1949	combine	blat glass	*	*			Fines totalling $44,000
1949	combine	matches	*	*			Fines totalling $85,000

SOURCE: Skeoch, 1966a.

TABLE 7-4.   GOVERNMENT COMBINES ACTIVITY 1950-1959 LEGISLATION

Year	Charge¹	Industry	Report Published	Decision			Penalty
				Convicted	Acquitted	No Action	
1952	combine	rubber	*	*			Fines of $220,000
1952	combine	bread	*			*	
1952	combine	fine paper	*	*			Fines of $242,000
1953	combine	coarse paper	*	*			Fines of $58,000
1953	combine	maple products	*			*	
1953	combine	electrical wire and cable	*	*			Fines of $82,000
1953	r.p.m.	soap	*			*	
1953	price dis.	retail hardware dealers	*			*	
1953	r.p.m.	household supplies	*	*			Individual salesman fined
1954	combine	gasoline	*		*		
1954	r.p.m.	china	*	*			Fines of $1,000
1954	r.p.m.	T.V. sets	*			*	
1954	combine	wire fencing	*	*			Fines of $60,000
1954	combine	coal	*	*			Fines varied $100 to $1,000
1955	m.,m.,t.	beer	*		*		
1955	combine	tar roofings	*	*			Fines of $110,000
1955	r.p.m.	appliances	*	*			Fine of $500
1955	combine	transmission equipment	*	*			Fines of $52,000
1956	combine	coal	*	*			Fines of $20,000
1956	combine	quilted goods	*	*			Fines of $6,500
1956	combine	paperboard	*	*			Fines of $65,000
1957	m.,m.,t.	tobacco	*			*	Association disbanded
1957	combine	metal culverts	*	*			Fines of $65,000
1957	m.,m.,t.	sugar	*		*		
1958	combine	pulpwood	*	*			Fines of $240,000

			Convicted	Acquitted	No Action	
1958	m.,m.,t.	yeast	*		*	
1958	m.,m.,t.	zinc	*		*	
1958	pred., pricing	confectionary items	*		*	
1959	monopoly	ammunition	*		*	
1959	combine	electrical materials	*	*		Fines of $15,000
1959	r.p.m.	surgical supplies	*	*		Fine of $300

¹ The following abbreviations for various charges will be used; r.p.m.—resale price maintenance; pric dis. = price discrimination; m.,m.,t. = combines, alleged merger, monopoly, trust; pred. pricing = predatory pricing
SOURCE: Skeoch, 1966a.

TABLE 7-5.   GOVERNMENT COMBINES ACTIVITY 1960-1972 LEGISLATION[a]

Year	Charge	Industry	Convicted	Acquitted	No Action	Penalty
1960	combine	sugar	*			Fines totalling $75,000
1960	r.p.m.	gasoline		*		
1960	combine	specialty bags			*	
1960	combine	coal	*			Fines totalling $46,500
1960	merger	newspapers			*	
1960	combine	packaging			*	
1960	combine	belts	*			Fine of $300
1961	price dis.	gasoline			*	
1961	price dis.	gasoline			*	
1961	price dis.	gasoline			*	
1961	r.p.m.	photo equip.	*			Order of Prohibition
1961	merger	meat packing			*	
1961	r.p.m.	cameras	*			Order of Prohibition
1961	combine	paper	*			Fines totalling $391,500

TABLE 7-5 (cont.)

Year	Charge	Industry	Convicted	Acquitted	No Action	Penalty
1962	merger	paper			*	
1962	merger	paper			*	
1962	pred. pricing	milk	*			
1962	r.p.m.	electric shavers	*			Fines totalling $4,000
1962[b]	r.p.m.	filters	*			Fine of $1,500
1963	combine	tenders	*			Fines totalling $3,000
1964	combine	plumbing/heating supplies	*			Fines totalling $57,500
1964	monopoly	newspapers		*		
1964[b]	r.p.m.	gasoline	*			Order of Prohibition
1964[b]	combine	ice cream	*			Order of Prohibition
1964	combine	plumbing supplies	*			Fines totalling $60,000
1964	combine	road materials		*		
1964	combine	milk		*		
1964	combine	pencils	*			Fines totalling $16,000
1965	merger/ monop.	propane			*	
1965	merger/ monop.	newspapers			*	
1965	combine	ashphalt mixes				Fines totalling $9,000
1965[b]	ind. inquiry	impeding				Fine of $3,500
1965	combine	plumbing/heating supplies			*	
1965[b]	impeding inquiry	K. J. Beamish				Fines of $3,500
1965	merger/ monop.	weed killer	*			Order of Prohibition
1966	price dis. & r.p.m.	knitting wool	*			Order of Prohibition

TABLE 7-5 (cont.)

1966	combine	concrete	*		Fines totalling $13,500
1966[b]	r.p.m.	skis	*		Order of Prohibition
1966	r.p.m.	gasoline		*	
1966[b]	combine	truck operators	*		Fines totalling $1,000
1966	merger/ monop.	chemicals	*		Fine/merger = $40,000; monop. = charge dropped
1966[b]	r.p.m.	W. E. Coutts Co. Ltd.	*		Fines totalling $500
1966[b]	combine	mandarin oranges	*		Fines totalling $98,500
1966[b]	combine	towels	*		Fines totalling $17,500
1966[b]	r.p.m.	electronics	*		Fines totalling $1,000
1967	r.p.m.	eggs	*		Order of Prohibition
1967	merger/ monop.	iron	*		Order of Prohibition
1967	combine	timber	*		Fines totalling $12,500
1967	r.p.m.	glassware	*		Fines totalling $3,200
1967[b]	combine	freight	*		Fines totalling $20,000
1968	combine	milk	*		Order of Prohibition
1968	combine	cloth	*		Fines totalling $20,000
1968	combine	flooring	*		Fines totalling $16,000
1969[b]	r.p.m.	N/A	*		Fine totalling $1,200
1969[b]	r.p.m.	skis	*		Fines totalling $7,900
1969[b]	combine	meat	*		Fines totalling $35,000
1969[b]	r.p.m.	gasoline		*	
1969[b]	r.p.m.	cosmetics	*		Fines totalling $750

TABLE 7-5 (cont.)

Year	Charge	Industry	Convicted	Acquitted	No Action	Penalty
1969[b]	combine	books	*			Order of Prohibition
1969[b]	combine	books	*			Order of Prohibition
1970	combine	paving			*	
1970[b]	combine	plaster	*			Fines totalling $75,000
1970[b]	r.p.m.	cosmetics	*			Fines totalling $1,000
1970	combine	printing				Verdict undecided
1970	combine	tenders			*	
1970	combine	metal products				Verdict undecided
1970[b]	combine	prescription drugs	*			Fines totalling $10,000
1970[b]	combine/ r.p.m.	electric lamps				Verdict undecided
1971[b]	monopoly	diaper service	*			Order of Prohibition
1971[b]	combine	glass fibre	*			Order of Prohibition
1971[b]	combine	stove oil	*			Order of Prohibition
1971[b]	combine	gasoline	*			Order of Prohibition
1971[b]	r.p.m.	automobiles		*		
1971[b]	r.p.m.	stereos	*			Fines totalling $2,000
1972[b]	combine	concrete	*			Fines totalling $245,000
1972[b]	pred. pricing	photo supplies	*			Order of Prohibition
1972[b]	combine	cement	*			Order of Prohibition
1972	combine	beer			*	

TABLE 7-5 (cont.)

1972[b]	combine	gasoline	*	Fines totalling $1,500
1972[b]	r.p.m.	chemicals	*	Order of Prohibition
1972[b]	r.p.m.	chemicals	*	Order of Prohibition
1972[b]	combine	chemicals	*	Order of Prohibition
1972[b]	r.p.m.	humidifiers	*	
1972[b]	r.p.m.	soil fumigants	*	Fines totalling $1,500
1972[b]	monopoly	food products		*

[a] All reports were considered published except for the 1962 r.p.m. case regarding filters.
[b] Referred directly to the Attorney General of Canada.
SOURCE: Canada, 1973.

TABLE 7-6.   CASES UNDER THE COMBINES INVESTIGATION ACT—
            MISLEADING ADVERTISING

Year	Number of Cases	Convictions	Acquittals
1962	6	5	1
1963	6	3	3
1964	2	1	1
1965	5	5	0
1966	6	6	0
1967	5	5	0
1968	16	14	2
1969	22	19	3
1970	45	37	8
1971	80	65	15
1972	89	74	15
TOTALS	282	234	48

SOURCE: Canada, 1973.

TABLE 7-7.   OPERATIONS OF THE BUREAU OF COMPETITION POLICY EXCLUDING MISLEADING ADVERTISING 1954-55 to 1971-72

	54–55	55–56	56–57	57–58	58–59	59–60	60–61	61–62	62–63	63–64	64–65	65–66	66–67	67–68	68–69	69–70	70–71	71–72	Total
1. Number of files opened on receipt of complaints or inquiries of the nature of complaints	96	91	48	77	127	113	152	232	239	134	131	117	117	97	107	141	255	271	2,545
2. Formal inquiries in progress at the end of the year	14	17	20	30	31	32	35	47	48	54	47	47	54	59	57	76	83	86	827
3. Preliminary inquiries of an extensive nature	*	*	*	*	*	*	44	42	42	29	10	23	19	19	15	28	17	30	318
4. Research projects in progress at end of year	3	3	3	4	3	4	3	3	3	1	1	1	3	2	2	4	2	3	48
5. Research projects completed	*	*	*	*	*	*	*	*	*	*	0	0	2	2	0	0	2	0	4
6. Investigations disposed of by reports of discontinuance to the Minister	7	2	2	3	10	13	13	11	18	24	22	10	22	15	19	4	9	17	221

* Information not collected.
SOURCE: Annual Report, Director of Combines Branch, 1961, 1964, 1974.

level of concentration in the economy is important in understanding the full extent of competition, or lack of it, because it "measures the absence of competition and the ease with which dominant firms can administer prices and mutually participate in exploitive market practices without fear of challenge."[6] Possible results of concentration in the economy include "strong market power, low competitive pressure, inefficiency, and poor resource allocation."[7] Concentration in a market can thus be viewed as a possible violation of combines laws in the form of a monopoly. "This trend toward monopoly and concentration has been actively encouraged by the federal government over the years, especially by the minister of finance, who has to approve each merger application personally."[8]

A primary mechanism leading to concentration in the business community is the merger, whereby numerous small companies join together to form one, dominant firm, or when an already existing dominant firm is able to buy out or in various other ways eliminate competitors. Mergers may, of course, be illegal under the Combines Act depending, as do monopolies, upon whether they restrict competition to the detriment of the consumer. Chart 7-1 shows the number of mergers, by year since 1900, in those areas under the regulation of the Combines Act. It illustrates the fact that an unprecedented number of mergers have occurred since 1960, with over half of the total number of mergers since 1900 taking place in this relatively short, thirteen-year span. Chart 7-2 denotes the value of assets acquired in comparison to the total number of mergers, 1945-1961, according to a detailed government study of combines during this time period which was released in 1969.

Table 7-8 points out the prosecution and conviction record of the Canadian government *vis-à-vis* mergers. It shows the number of mergers based on the terms of the various combines acts, the number of mergers charged by the federal government as being illegal according to combines laws, and the number of mergers convicted by the Combines Branch, 1900-1972. Prior to 1960, no mergers were successfully prosecuted by the government, while, after this date, of the 3572 mergers, only nine mergers have been prosecuted and only three have been convicted. In these three convictions, the penalty has twice been an Order of Prohibition, and once a fine of $40 000. Thus, since 1923, when mergers became violations under the new combines legislation, only .003% of the total number of mergers have been charged as

---

6 Don Mitchell, *The Politics of Food* (Toronto: James Lorimer and Company, 1975), p. 35.

7 Economic Council of Canada, *Interim Report on Competition Policy* (Ottawa: Information Canada, 1969), p. 70.

8 Donald Gutstein, *Vancouver Ltd.* (Toronto: James Lorimer and Company, 1975), p. 31.

violations of the combines laws, and only .0005% of the mergers in this same time period have been successfully convicted.

This great number of mergers has resulted in the creation of greatly concentrated industrial sectors, dominated by a relatively few major corporations. When no more than four firms control 50% or more of a specific market, they are in a dominant position, and non-competitive activity on the part of these firms becomes the norm. Some examples of these industries are automobiles, cigarettes, break-fast cereals and various home appliances.

While over 170 000 active corporations[9] exist in the Canadian business community, the ones that the Combines Branch takes an interest in are those relatively few which can engage in non-competitive behaviour. The cost of this behaviour to the public reaches enormous proportions, as dominant firms are able to restrict output in

FIGURE 7-1.   NUMBER OF MERGERS, BY YEAR, 1900-1972

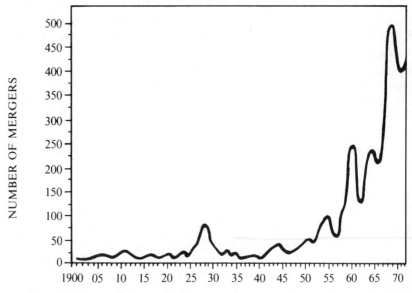

SOURCE: Skeoch, 1966a; Canada, 1969; Young, 1974.

___

9 Department of Consumer and Corporate Affairs, *Concentration in the Manufacturing Industries of Canada* (Ottawa, 1971), p. 13. The report states that, of these nearly 170,000 active corporations in Canada, approximately 167,000 had assets valued at less than $5 million.

FIGURE 7-2.   MERGER ACTIVITY IN CANADA, 1945-1961

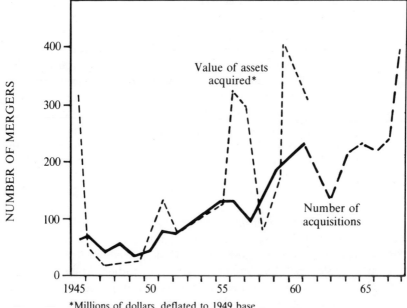

*Millions of dollars, deflated to 1949 base

SOURCE: Canada, 1969:84.

TABLE 7-8.   MERGERS, MERGERS PROSECUTED, AND MERGERS
CONVICTED BY CANADIAN COMBINES LEGISLATION, 1900-
1972

| *Legislation* | *Mergers* | | | | |
	Total Number	*Number Prosecuted*	*Per Cent Prosecuted*	*Number Convicted*	*Per Cent Convicted*
1900-1909	47	0	0.000	0	0.000
1910-1922	160	0	0.000	0	0.000
1923-1934	416	1	0.002	0	0.000
1935-1936	28	0	0.000	0	0.000
1937-1951	359	1	0.003	0	0.000
1952-1960	1174	5	0.004	0	0.000
1960-1972	3572	9	0.003	3	0.001
TOTALS	5756	16	0.003	3	0.005

SOURCE: Skeoch, 1966a; Weldon, 1966; Canada, 1973.

order to maintain or increase profits; true competition would lower profits. A staff report by the Federal Trade Commission in the United States estimates that "if highly concentrated industries were deconcentrated to the point where the four largest firms control forty percent or less of an industry's sales, prices would fall by twenty-five percent or more."[10] Other Trade Commission studies in the cereal industry bear this statement out: prices of these products are between 15% and 25% higher than they would be with competition because four firms dominate the industry. Another study in the United States attempted to place a figure on the cost of lost output as a result of dominant firms overpricing their products. It concluded that the cost of monopoly in terms of lost production was between $48 billion and $60 billion annually.[11] It has been estimated that lost output as a result of monopoly in Canada is about 10% of the U.S. figure—$4.5 to $6.0 billion annually.[12]

In Canada, both government reports, and studies by economists and sociologists, have revealed invaluable information concerning the state of concentration in those areas of the economy governed by combines legislation. More importantly, those studies provide evaluation, almost decade by decade, of the Combines Branch's efforts to restrict anti-competitive actions by members of the business community and to protect the practice of competition for the public.

As early as 1934, indications were that a high degree of concentration existed in various sectors of the Canadian economy. The Communist Party of Canada, in a brief submitted to the Royal Commission on Dominion-Provincial Relations, pointed out that between 1930-1934, 75% of the net profits of corporations were earned by only 349 corporations, but that thirty-five of them made 50% of all net profits for the same period.[13] During the 1934-35 period, the Royal Commission on Price Spreads determined that a high degree of concentration existed in eight of the ten selected industries under study.[14]

---

10 Max Green, "The High Cost of Monopoly," in *Superconcentration/ Supercorporation*, ed., Ralph Andreano (Andover, Massachusetts: Warner Modular Publications, Incorporation, 1973).

11 Cy Gonick, *Inflation or Depression* (Toronto: James Lorimer and Company, 1975), p. 22. In addition, Gonick points out that monopoly leads to numerous social problems (p. 22).

12 *Ibid.*

13 Bert Young, "Corporate Interests and the State," *Our Generation*, 10 (Winter-Spring, 1974), pp. 70-83. Reprinted from *Our Generation* magazine, 3934 St. Urbain St., Montreal, Canada.

14 Royal Commission on Dominion-Provincial Relations 1938, cited in V. W. Bladen, "Canada," in *Monopoly and Competition and Their Regulation*, ed., E. Chamberlin (London: Macmillan and Company, 1954), pp. 8-10.

Studies in 1948 revealed a continued strong tendency toward a monopolistic situation.

A study on concentration in Canadian manufacturing industries
between the years of 1948 and 1950 by Rosenbluth led him to con-
clude that:

*...9 or less of the leading firms account for 80 percent of employment,
and in one-third of the industries less than 5 firms account for 80 percent
employment. Examples of industries with very high concentration are the
primary metals, automobiles, railway equipment, cotton textiles, cigarettes, distilleries, and many of the industries processing nonmetalic
minerals and chemicals.*[15]

Porter, studying concentration for the same years as did Rosenbluth, found that:

*...183 dominant corporations were responsible for 40 to 50 percent of
the gross value of production in manufacturing, 90 percent of railway
transportation, 63 percent of the total value of metal production, 88
percent of the gross earnings of the telegraph and cable service....*[16]

A government study of concentration in the manufacturing industries in 1965 found that 174 corporations had 50% of corporate assets.
The largest fifty manufacturing corporations, each having assets of
$100 million and over, accounted for 40.1% of the total manufacturing
assets, 31.8% of total sales, and 45.9% of total profits. In the mining
sector, only sixteen companies had assets of $100 million and over;
yet, they controlled 37.2% of total mining assets, 44.5% of total sales,
and 46.1% of total profits. Seventeen of the largest utilities accounted
for 72.7% of total assets in the sector, and eighty of the finance,
insurance, and real estate corporations accounted for 61.7% of total
assets in their own sector.[17]

The latest government figures concerning concentration in Canadian industries are shown in Table 7-9, in which statistics for 1970 and
1971 concerning selected industrial sectors of the Canadian economy
are compared. While it appears that a few more companies share the
"wealth" of the Canadian economy in 1971 than in 1970, one must
wait for a long-term trend to develop before arguing that corporate
wealth is becoming decentralized.

15 Young, "Corporate Interests and the State," p. 76.
16 John Porter, *The Vertical Mosaic* (Toronto: The University of Toronto Press, 1965),
    p. 233.
17 Consumer and Corporate Affairs, *Concentration in the Manufacturing Industries in
    Canada*, pp. 13-15.

TABLE 7-9.   NUMBER OF CORPORATIONS BY ASSET SIZE IN CANADA, FOR SELECTED INDUSTRIAL SECTORS, 1970 AND 1971

Sector	1970					1971				
	Total	Corporations with Assets of $25 Million or More		Corporations with Assets of $100 Million or More		Total	Corporations with Assets of $25 Million or More		Corporations with Assets of $100 Million or More	
		Number	% Total	Number	% Total		Number	% Total	Number	% Total
1. Agriculture, Forestry and Fishing	6 353	3	*	0	*	7 022	3	*	0	*
2. Mining	3 735	97	75	30	52	3 740	106	76	34	54
3. Mfg.	22 084	271	53	74	34	21 998	280	55	83	35
4. Construc'n.	19 974	21	*	2	*	21 293	25	*	2	*
5. Utilities	8 823	98	82	44	65	9 062	103	75	46	63
6. Finance	75 438	309	91	97	86	78 688	338	91	108	87
7. Wholesale Trade	24 844	38	25	6	14	25 099	53	24	8	12
8. Retail Trade	32 327	28	24	9	16	33 851	28	26	10	17
9. Services	28 664	17	10	—	—	30 783	23	11	0	0
TOTALS (all sectors)	222 835	882	69	262	60	231 536	959	70	291	61

* Information not available.
SOURCE: Statistics Canada, Corporation Financial Statistics, 1971.

The Director of Investigation in the Combines Branch between 1960 and 1972, the period of continued monopolistic situations and of the greatest merger activity in Canada's history, was D. W. Henry. Although he had the power to investigate these mergers and their effect upon both the economy and public, his personal opinion of big business was similar to Mackenzie King's—investigate and prosecute only those who "misuse" their power. It was this pro-business attitude which led him to establish a close contact with the Canadian Manufacturers' Association and other corporate lobbies to help them to understand combines legislation. Particularly in the area of mergers, Henry was active in informing businessmen "off the record" about whether their proposed mergers would be illegal under the Combines Act. "Henry cannot guarantee his advice will be upheld in the courts. But he can claim that never has he advised a firm which proceeded accordingly, and then found itself on the wrong end of a combines act court judgement."[18]

Thus, while on the public payroll and entrusted with powers to investigate possible illegal acts under the Combines Act, Henry was freely interpreting and giving legal advice to the businesses he was supposed to be investigating and prosecuting! As the yearly report of the Director of Investigation in 1965 pointed out, Henry considered this to be an essential function of his position as director, and freely used research resources and government monies to aid businesses.

In past Annual Reports of the Director reference has been made to a policy of encouraging businessmen to discuss frankly the application of the Act to their problems. One area of response to this policy has been the confidential disclosure of proposed mergers requesting an opinion from the Director whether or not in the particular circumstances he would feel obliged to commence an inquiry if the proposed merger were to proceed. In most cases a substantial amount of factual information and research may be required before it is possible to develop an informed view of a proposed merger and the examination of such proposals may take on many aspects of an inquiry although formal powers of obtaining information have not been used at this stage.[19]

By 1968, Henry felt sure that he had succeeded in winning the confidence of big business, thereby *improving his department's image in their eyes.* In his informal investigations of proposed mergers, he assured big business that "bigness didn't mean badness". Writing in the *Financial Post* in 1968 he stated that

18 Mitchell, *The Politics of Food*, p. 181.
19 Annual Report of the Director of Investigation, Combines Branch, 1965, p. 41.

*more than 2500 mergers have taken place in Canada in the post-war
period and of these not more than a handful has been challenged by the
director of investigation and research and <u>none has been struck down
by the courts</u>. . . . Look at the 100 largest Canadian firms. A number of
them have been convicted for conspiracy, but a restrictive agreement can
scarcely be called bigness. None has been convicted of a merger, or
monopoly offense or of predatory pricing*[20] *[emphasis added]*.

Yet the Restrictive Trade Practices Commission had discovered
illegal mergers among many top corporations, as shown in Table 7-10.
The reality of the situation was that government lawyers couldn't
secure a conviction in most instances because of the loopholes and
escape clauses in the Combines Act. Henry was serving the interests of
big business. Instead of tightening up the legislation to secure more
convictions, he remained a confidant to those interests opposite to the
publicly-stated philosophy and code of the Combines Act, leaving the
existing laws ineffective and unenforceable.

Combines Administration Expenditures and Size of Staff

Combatting the illegal activities of corporations under the Combines
Act requires large expenditures and a large staff to investigate and
gather evidence if convictions against the large corporations, which
have large assets and profits as well as numerous lawyers, are to be
secured. Expenditures and staff size are important indicators in determining the government's real intentions of enforcing combines laws.
Table 7-11 illustrates the total amount of expenditures by the Combines Branch, 1936-1972. In comparing these figures with other government departments, in the fiscal year 1959/60 it has been pointed
out that some other expenditures on other government operations
included, in millions of dollars, 2.3 for the Canadian Government
Travel Bureau, Research in Agricultural Economics (0.7), and New-
foundland Bait Commission (0.5), compared to the roughly half-mil-
lion-dollar expenditure of the Combines Branch.[21] By 1972, while
combines expenditures exceeded two million dollars, the Government
Travel Bureau spent (in millions of dollars) 11.1, and Class "A" and
Class "B" Agricultural Fairs received 1.1 from the federal government.
As Rosenbluth and Thorburn commented, "if . . . anti-combines activity
were considered necessary, expenditures could be increased four or

20 *Ibid.*, p. 181.
21 Rosenbluth and Thorburn, *Canadian Anti-Combines Legislation*, p. 44.

TABLE 7-10. REPORTS OF MERGERS AND MONOPOLIES DEFINED AS
ILLEGAL BUT NO ACTION TAKEN 1960-1968

Year	Industry	Remarks
1961	Outdoor advertising	Previous director had recommended prosecution, but new director dropped proceedings.
	Newspapers	Southam Co. (total assets in 1961, $27 million) acquired three newspapers in Vancouver, the merger was allowed on the condition that present policy was not altered.
1962	Meat Packing	Both Canada Packers and Burns Company were active in mergers.
1963	Forest Products	MacMillan Bloedel Ltd., largest firm in British Columbia buys out Power River Corporation, second largest producer of forest products in B.C.
1964	Chemicals	Canadian Celanese Ltd., merger with Canadian Chemical Co.
	Steel	Four firms merged to form largest corporation in industry.
1965	Newspapers	Thomson Ltd. (total assets in 1961, $20 million) buys out the only two papers in Fort William, Ont., but director felt there was still competition from outside area.
1967	Food Processing	
	Food Wholesalers	Company acquired 50% of fruit market in Ontario, but insufficient evidence to prosecute.
1968	Propane Gas	
	Bell Telphone	Bell acquires all the private telephone companies in Eastern Canada, but the director only notes that he is concerned.

SOURCE: Young, 1974:79.

five times without a significant impact on the government's finances."[22] Table 7-11 also illustrates that federal authorities, in contrast to their support of combines enforcement, spend much more money for controlling street crime (in 1972, approximately sixty times as much money to support the Royal Canadian Mounted Police law enforcement program).

While Table 7-12 shows an impressive increase in the number of staff in the Combines Branch—over 500% for total staff, and close to 600% for research staff—these figures are in reality small compared to the increase in research and investigation they have to do; for example, the increase in the number of mergers alone between 1960 and 1972 would greatly tax the increase in both staff and expenditures, given the previously noted need for more extensive investigation in this area.

TABLE 7-11.   COMBINES INVESTIGATION EXPENDITURE 1936-1972

| Fiscal Year | Total Expenditure by Combines Branch | | RCMP Law Enforcement Programme[a] |
| | A | B | |
	$000	$000	$000
1936	3.4		
1937			
1938	14.6		
1939	52.5		
1940	45.3		
1941	61.8		
1942	57.5		
1943	23.4		
1944	25.2		
1945	24.9		
1946	34.6		
1947	77.6		
1948	124.8		
1949	169.4		
1950	168.8		
1951	221.1		
1952	215.8		
1953	267.0		

22 *Ibid.*, pp. 44-45.

1954	393.7	329.2	
1955	407.5	328.1	
1956	426.5	361.5	
1957	427.9	360.3	
1958	372.9	319.9	
1959	394.2	340.6	
1960	541.9	475.4	
1961	547.3	440.7	
1962	538.9	443.8	
1963	564.5	468.8	56 908.4
1964	604.5	502.1	64 656.4
1965	707.2	601.6	63 868.0
1966	825.2	713.0	64 360.2
1967	1 022.9	919.9	62 803.0
1968	1 171.5	1 048.6	61 849.6
1969	1 194.4	1 083.5	74 215.2
1970	1 501.9	1 387.2	81 667.3
1971	1 619.7	1 533.0	101 525.8
1972	2 149.3	2 058.2	120 144.5

[a] These figures include national police services, federal law enforcement agencies, and provincial and municipal policing under contract.
A: Total Expenditure. B: Expenditure for the Director of Investigation and Research (from 1954).
SOURCE: Rosenbluth and Thorburn, 1964:46, and Department of Finance, Public Accounts, 1961-1972.

This great increase in expenditures and staff by the Combines Branch is not as significant as one would tend to think when compared to the increase in general economic activity:

When viewed against the background of the great increase in general economic activity . . . the increase in the volume of anti-combines work looks less spectacular. The rate at which investigations are undertaken increased greatly, but so did the number of situations that should be investigated, so that the relative effectiveness of the investigative machinery rose by much less than the increased expenditure might suspect . . . it may be concluded that with the establishment of the new machinery (in 1960) the resources devoted to the administration of the act increased, as did the amount of activity under the act. Subsequent expansion . . . did not keep pace with the growth of the economy and of other government activities. . . . [23]

23 *Ibid.*, pp. 50, 55.

TABLE 7-12.   NUMBER OF STAFF, COMBINES BRANCH 1957-1972

Fiscal Year	Total Staff, Director of Investigation and Research	Research Officers	Per Cent of Research Officers to Total Staff	Total Staff, Restrictive Trade Practices Commission[b]
1957	59	16	27.5	7
1958	61	16	26.2	5
1959	61	17	27.9	5
1960	62	17	27.4	7
1961	70	20	28.6	8
1962	72	21	29.2	6
1963	73	22	30.1	8
1964	83	25	30.1	8
1965	81	23	28.4	8
1966	88	26	29.5	8
1967	106	30	28.3	9
1968	133	44	33.1	8
1969	140	49	35.0	7
1970	140	51	36.4	6
1971	201	73	36.3	5
1972	262	100	38.2	5

[a] The figures for Total Staff include Research Officers.
[b] The figures include clerical staff.

Conclusion

It appears that, through this empirical evaluation of the government's "record" of enforcement of the Combines Act, the conclusions reached at the end of Chapters 5 and 6 have been largely borne out. It has solidified the position that the government is not a neutral body, but rather is susceptible to the interests of powerful economic groups. The various indicators examined in this chapter not only call into question the government's professed intentions based upon its own record of performance, but also show the low priority given to support of the Combines Branch by the federal government.

Examining the rate of prosecutions and convictions in only one of the areas under the jurisdiction of the Combines Act, namely mergers, suggests that other acts considered illegal, e.g., price discrimination, occur many times more than the low enforcement record in each specific area shows. The increase in prosecutions and convictions in most areas over the past few years may be insignificant when compared to the reality of the situation, as the example of mergers readily illustrates. Moreover, both the size of staff and the amount of financial aid received by the Combines Branch are important in deterring illegal activity but, while they have increased recently, the Branch has not generally been successful as an agency of control.

Penalties have also been insufficient as a deterrent, with the possible financial rewards for companies entering into restraint of trade agreements far outweighing the possible loss as a result of fines imposed by the government. The government has usually issued "Order of Prohibition" penalties, rather than fining the offender or issuing other penalties, such as lowering the tariff duties on foreign products to compensate the Canadian consumer by way of increasing competition. In addition, while officers of various companies have been charged with separate offences under the Combines Investigation Act, they are usually fined, even though the combines laws have always contained a separate provision for sentencing individuals. However, no individual has ever been sent to jail for a combines offence.

Further, it can be derived from this chapter that even if new, strict measures of regulation and enforcement were instituted, and a rapid increase in size of staff and amount of financial aid occurred, the action would be too late. That is, a high degree of concentration would continue to exist in the Canadian economy, thereby robbing the new legislation of any immediate effect for the public. Nonetheless, various changes may ultimately provide better control of corporate crime.

CHAPTER 8

Suite Crime and Social Policy

If criminal law is to be a respected force in society, it is important that these acts not be treated more leniently than anti-social acts in the streets. To ignore, for example, evidence of fraud or corruption in corporations, to ignore deliberate or even careless action that threatens to destroy order within the economy, can create the dangerous impression that people and groups controlling economic power are beyond the law.

Law Reform Commission of Canada, *Criminal Responsibility for Group Action* (Ottawa: Information Canada, 1976), p. 65.

The commonly stated reasons for the use of criminal law include rehabilitation, restraint, deterrence, symbolism and retribution.[1] These varied and sometimes contradictory purposes are usually the basis for determining the disposition of the accused and the sentencing of convicted offenders. The Law Reform Commission of Canada has completed a report on this topic which addressed the straightforward question of "How should we treat those who offend against us?"[2] While the range of dispositions and sentences recommended by the commission is quite broad in order to maintain maximum flexibility, the report concerns itself with individual violations, rather than group violations, i.e., illegal behaviour by corporations. To rectify this omission, the Law Reform Commission completed a report on *Criminal Responsibility for Group Action* which addresses the issue of crime by corporations.[3] The following discussion will first concern itself with individual culpability and then with group (corporate) culpability. Both of these aspects of corporate crime will be addressed in terms of the goals of the law and the dispositions and sentences recommended by the Law Reform Commission.[4]

Corporate Criminals

While our investigation has emphasized criminal corporations and group responsibility, individual responsibility and corporate responsibility are interrelated. The legal responsibility of individuals for the behaviour of corporations is found through two approaches.[5] First are traditional criminal charges, such as fraud, theft, violence, and intimidation—individual criminal acts which may be performed through corporations. Secondly, corporate officers, directors and agents may be liable for offences committed by corporations through statutory provisions naming such positions as criminally responsible. The traditional offences are those for which individuals are prosecuted and found

---

1 Gwynn Nettler, *Explaining Crime* (New York: McGraw-Hill Book Company, 1974), pp. 32-35.
2 The Law Reform Commission of Canada, *Dispositions and Sentences in the Criminal Process* (Ottawa: Information Canada, 1976), p. 1.
3 Law Reform, *Criminal ... Action.*
4 Our discussion of policy will only touch upon those aspects of the Stage Two Proposals for a New Competition Policy which are directly pertinent to our suggested remedies. For a specific, detailed description of the Stage Two proposals see *Proposals for a New Competition Policy for Canada: Second Stage.* (Ottawa: Consumer and Corporate Affairs, 1977). Unfortunately, many of our suggestions are entirely overlooked by the proposed legislation.
5 Law Reform Commission of Canada, *Criminal ... Action,* p. 6.

guilty, while the latter category of individual responsibility is rarely used. As noted in Chapter 7, Table 7-2, most of the convictions for violations of the Combines Act are of companies and corporations, rather than individuals. Furthermore, when individuals have been convicted, fines have resulted. "The combines law has always contained separate provision for the sentencing of individuals; and while no individual in Canada has ever been sent to jail for a combines offence, officers and independent entrepreneurs have occasionally been fined."[6]

Because it is rarely used against individual corporate criminals, little is known about the effectiveness of the criminal law when applied to corporate criminals. Thus community crime prevention programs, such as Neighbourhood Watch, are aimed at common crimes and common criminals. Police-community programs which emphasize vigilance concerning corporate crime are yet to be realized. Policing of the Combines Act is essentially carried out by employees of the Department of Consumer and Corporate Affairs with the assistance of citizen's complaints. Discretion undoubtedly is used with regard to the decision to ask the Director to investigate further a possible violation. Ultimately, it is the Director who determines whether more investigation is needed, charges should be filed, etc. Thus, the Director, and before him, the field staff, play a role in screening cases similar to that of the policeman and prosecutor.

The Director, as noted in Chapter 7, has proceeded very cautiously in bringing charges against corporations. Rosenbluth and Thorburn have pointed out that charges are not laid unless there is an excellent chance of conviction based upon legal criteria.[7] Even with this caution, the conviction rate has been 63%, with 7% acquittals, 27% no action taken and 2% still pending based on 190 prosecutions. Since only 126 reports have been published during the time span covered by our analysis, there may be need for further manpower and other support mechanisms to police corporations and corporate criminals. While there is much attention given to policing the streets, the money and personnel needed to police the suites is pitifully lacking. Besides increasing the size and abilities of investigating agencies, it may be useful to use undercover agents in corporations in order to detect corporate criminals.

Deterrence is often heralded as a major (if not the major) goal of the use of the criminal law, therefore, we should look at this aspect of

6 Bruce C. McDonald, "Criminality and the Canadian Anti-Combines Laws", *Alberta Law Review*, 4 (1965), p. 77.

7 G. Rosenbluth and H. Thorburn, *Canadian Anti-Combines Legislation, 1952-1960* (Toronto: University of Toronto Press, 1963).

social control. Students of crime generally agree that the threat and/or application of legal sanctions is potentially more effective as a deterrent for instrumental rather than expressive crimes.[8] In the latter category are a large proportion of such crimes as murder, sexual assault, and illicit drug use which are often situational, emotive and oriented to immediate needs. Instrumental crimes, on the other hand, fit more readily into the "rational man" model of human behaviour which underlies the rationale for using the penal sanction.[9] Since corporate crime fits the instrumental model, theoretically the use of a sanction should have a deterrent effect, assuming the criminal has relative certainty of detection, apprehension, and conviction and the penalty is sufficiently severe to counter the gains obtained by committing the act. As one student of crime observes: "The deeds of people in complex organizations struggling in a competitive, profit-making situation are neither accidental nor unpredictable, but emanate naturally from the functional situation and should be taken into account by decision makers, whether in management or government."[10]

While there is a growing body of literature concerning the impact of legal sanctions as a deterrent, most of the attention has been paid to common crimes in general and violent crimes specifically, particularly to assessments of the effect of the death penalty on murder rates.[11] Limited study of the imposition of legal sanctions upon corporate criminals has been undertaken.[12] This is due to both the very small number of individuals who have been sanctioned, and the lack of official societal concern regarding this type of crime.

When individual corporate criminals have appeared in court, fines have been the most severe sanction. The levying of fines against corporate criminals has been criticized due to their small nature, the fact that they may be paid by the company, and/or the fact that they are not viewed negatively in the business world. It should be noted that the very low possibility of detection, apprehension and subsequent

8 William B. Banston and John A. Cramer, "Toward a Macro-Sociological Interpretation of General Deterrence," *Criminology*, 12 (November, 1974), pp. 251-80. Concerning subjective measures of deterrence see James J. Teevan, Jr., "Deterrent Effects of Punishment: Subjective Measures Continued," *Canadian Journal of Criminology and Corrections*, 18 (April, 1976), pp. 152-60.

9 Of course it must be noted that these are not mutually exclusive categories of crime. However, criminological literature supports the notion that certain types of crimes are more expressive and more instrumental than others. See Marshall B. Clinard and Richard Quinney, *Criminal Behaviour Systems: A Typology*, 2nd Edition (New York: Holt, Rinehart and Winston, 1973).

10 Leo Davids, "Penology and Corporate Crime," *Journal of Criminal Law, Criminology and Police Science*, 58 (December, 1967), pp. 526-27.

11 Banston and Cramer, "Toward ... Deterrence."

12 H. Posner, "A Statistical Study of Antitrust Enforcement," *Journal of Law and Economics*, 13 (1970), pp. 367-73.

conviction may largely negate any potential impact of fines or other sanctions.

While incarceration is a legal possibility, no one has ever been sent to jail for violations of combines laws.[13] Thus, the provision for stretches in jail seems to be largely symbolic of the *potential* harshness with which corporate criminals may be dealt, rather than serving the instrumental purpose of deterring offences by the *actual use* of this alternative. Professor Gilbert Geis, a leading authority on white collar crime, argues that such a sentence should be imposed for the purposes of deterrence, symbolism, and retribution.

I do not, however, find it incompatible to favor both a reduction of the lower-class prison population and an increase in upper-class representation in prisons. Jail terms have a self-evident deterrent impact upon corporate officials, who belong to a social group that is exquisitely sensitive to status deprivation and censure. The white-collar offender and his business colleagues, more than the narcotic addict or ghetto mugger, are apt to learn well the lesson intended by a prison term. In addition, there is something to be said for noblesse oblige, that those who have a larger share of what society offers carry a greater responsibility also.[14]

In terms of deterrence, it is easily argued that the use of such a penalty will stop the individual offender from committing further crimes of this nature and also deter others from such behaviour. Symbolically, it would represent the extreme disapproval of such behaviour by the public and would represent the equality of the law in terms of equal justice for all citizens. It has been noted that in Canada, the incarceration rate is higher than most other Western democracies of a similar size and level of industrialization and urbanization.[15] Few inmates of jails are white-collar criminals and none are violators of combines laws. Therefore, the perception of "common criminals" and others, that the law is biased in favour of the rich and powerful is a reality. As the Law Reform Commission states: "Our prison population, for example, contains a quite unrepresentative proportion of poor, of disadvantaged and of native offenders. The richer you are, the better your chance of getting away with something."[16]

---

13 McDonald, *Criminality*. It should be noted that a few corporate criminals have been sentenced to jail in the United States for violation of the Sherman Anti-Trust Act. See Gilbert Geis, ed., *White Collar Criminal* (New York: Atherton Press, 1968.)

14 Gilbert Geis, "Deterring Corporate Crime," in *The Criminologist: Crime and the Criminal*, ed., Charles E. Reasons (Pacific Palisades: Goodyear Publishing Company, 1974), p. 246.

15 Irwin Waller and Janet Chan, "Prison Use: A Canadian and International Comparison," *Criminal Law Quarterly*, 17 (December, 1974), pp. 47-71.

16 Law Reform Commission of Canada, *Our Criminal Law* (Ottawa: Information Canada, 1976), p. 12.

Finally, retribution has been, and will continue to be, an aim of the criminal law. By punishing the corporate criminal in a similar way to the common criminal, it provides the offender with his just deserts. As Geis suggests, those sharing in more of the benefits of society should also share a greater responsibility. Some possible consequences of sending fewer lower-class and more corporate criminals to jail are a "better class" of criminals, less violence, more obedience, fewer welfare families of prisoners, and the addition of technical and managerial skills for use by prison officials.[17]

Criminal Corporations

Nation-states have historically failed to regard corporations as subject to the criminal law. It is more difficult to talk about corporate behaviour, corporate thought, and corporate intent in traditional criminal law terms like individual responsibility, intent, etc. As discussed in Chapter 2, a cornerstone of contemporary criminal law is the individual, his actions, intentions and their meaning through interpretation.[18] Nonetheless, during the last century, courts and parliament have increasingly held that corporations should be liable for crimes of omission, and criminally responsible for nuisance, criminal negligence, criminal libel and contempt of court. Corporate employers, like human employers, may be held accountable for certain behaviour of their employees.[19] Finally, corporations can be held criminally responsible

17 For a discussion of some unintended consequences of current prisons see Charles E. Reasons and Russell L. Kaplan, "Tear Down the Walls? Some Functions of Prisons," *Crime and Delinquency*, 21 (October, 1975), pp. 360-72.

18 For a discussion of some of these issues see M. Goode, "Corporate Conspiracy: Problems of Mens Rea and the Parties to the Agreement," *The Dalhousie Law Journal*, 2 (February, 1975), pp. 121-56; McDonald, *Criminality*; Law Reform, *Criminal... Action.*

19 Law Reform, *Criminal... Action*, pp. 7-8. We would like to point out that this report distinguishes between "real crimes" and "regulatory offences" in discussing corporate crime. "Real crimes" are primarily concerned with fundamental values in society. Thus, laws regarding these values promote respect for the basic fiber of the social system. Such crimes are intentional offences with fault being specific. "Regulatory offences" are more concerned with behavioural results than societal values. Emphasis is upon obtaining conformity with regulations believed to be in the public intent or good. Fault and intention are less significant in such offences. These distinctions made by the Law Reform Commission appear to be similar to the classic distinctions made between wrongs which are *mala in se* (wrong in themselves) and *mala prohibita* (wrong because they intrude upon other's rights). See Nettler, *Explaining Crime*, pp. 35-36. However, such distinctions are often difficult to maintain in actual operation. For example, a corporation's lack of maintaining certain safety standards may be viewed legally as *mala prohibita* (regulatory offence), while the injuries and/or deaths which may be a consequence of such behaviour violate the "sacred" value of health and life. If honesty, fairness and competition are basic values in our society, then most, if not all, violations of the Combines Act are "real crimes." While this is our position, we recognize that

as a "person" for crimes which involve active wrongdoing. Therefore, two ways of holding corporations liable are available under current laws. One is based upon the doctrine of "vicarious responsibility" where a corporation is responsible for the behaviour of its agents and employees. In these cases strict liability is employed, thus, proof of fault is not necessary. The other major basis for corporate liability is regarding the corporation as an offender (person) and determining its fault through the fault of certain corporate officials. Of course, such a process is much easier in smaller corporations where responsibility is more concentrated. Also, smaller companies are more vulnerable due to participation in activities which are policed more heavily, rather than those which large corporations engage in, such as mergers and monopolies. Furthermore, smaller corporations are less likely to have the legal staff and/or political power to be an impressive foe of the Crown. Such factors undoubtedly contribute to the higher proportion of small corporations which are convicted of combines violations. Nonetheless, corporations should be held criminally responsible for harm emanating from their policies and/or practices.

It seems reasonable, in our view, that if criminal responsibility is to be placed on corporations, the harm resulting from the action or inaction on the part of people within the corporation should be related to the policies that are adopted by the corporation to achieve its objectives, the practices that may become accepted within the corporation, or the failure by corporate policy-makers to take steps to prevent its occurrence.[20]

The Law Reform Commission recommends that the burden of proof should be placed upon corporations to satisfy the court that alleged crime was not supported by the knowledge or intention of appropriate corporate officials.[21] However, it is suggested that the "defence of due diligence" be allowed, whereby the corporation presents the case that all reasonable care was taken to avoid the unfortunate consequence in regulatory offences.

Similar problems of detection, apprehension and conviction are found with criminal corporations as with corporate criminals. However, by maintaining that the corporation is responsible for certain behaviour, criminal law may be used where it is difficult to establish guilt of any one person. Emphasizing the individual is difficult with foreign-owned companies where the individual may not be liable

---

this is arguable, therefore, the distinction made by the Law Reform Commission is of little value to our presentation.

20 *Ibid.*, p. 20.
21 *Ibid.*, p. 22.

to Canadian law. Furthermore, by placing the corporation responsible, the criminal law is recognizing the significance of group behaviour and group process in the violation of laws, particularly in our highly organizationally complex society. Charging a corporation may help to provide better remedies through restitution for the victims of the behaviour. The Commission points out, however, that ultimately corporate responsibility is based upon the behaviour of specific individuals within the corporation; therefore, while criminal corporations should be subject to criminal sanctions, emphasis should be placed upon individual culpability in the corporate hierarchy. Although the saying "the buck stops here" has literal meaning for corporate officials in terms of their monetary gains, its meaning in terms of responsibility is more difficult to pinpoint in corporate behaviour.

The record of dispositions of criminal corporations is not much better than that of corporate criminals. Little effort has been made to police such behaviour and subsequent sanctions have been few. For example, while the area of mergers and concentration is within the purview of the Combines Act, the data in Chapter 7 show that little effort is being made to police this area.

Thus far, the sentencing of criminal corporations provides us with little encouragement in terms of the deterrent, symbolic and retributive effects of criminal law. As Chapter 6 noted, corporations convicted of violating combines laws were either fined and/or given an order of prohibition. A major problem with fines is that they are often small and unrelated to the harm inflicted and profit gained through the criminal behaviour. Thus, as a deterrent and/or retribution, current practices seem inadequate. One possibility is establishing the fine in relation to the harm caused. "The possibility exists of developing a formula for corporations to equalize the marginal deprivation imposed on each corporation by a fine in relation to such factors as profits, total assets, and ability to deflect the impact of the fine."[22]

Therefore, similar to proposals to fine individual offenders in proportion to their economic position, corporations could be fined in relation to their financial capacities. It has been argued that such fine schedules would be a more effective deterrent than increased probability of detection and conviction.[23] We believe that the combination of both increased policing of corporations and more severe penalties will most effectively contribute to deterring criminal corporations and their actors and providing them with the proper punishment. Such action

---

22 *Ibid.*, p. 38.
23 William Brent and Kenneth G. Elzinga, "Antitrust Penalties and Attitudes Toward Risk: An Economic Analysis," *Harvard Law Review*, 80 (1973), pp. 693-99.

will increase the symbolic significance of the professed equality of our legal system and support the statement that no one is above the law. Also, the court may strip the corporation of its profits and order restitution. While corporations cannot be incarcerated, their representatives can. Penalties as severe as incarceration which might be used against corporations include prohibition of certain activities, severe restrictions on the scope of corporate operations, and the elimination of the corporation from the business community.[24]

Mergers and Monopolies

As noted in Chapter 5, the Second Stage Proposals for a New Competition Policy in Canada present a major change in official government practice concerning mergers and monopolies. The government's philosophical position is largely based upon a background study by Skeoch and McDonald—economist and lawyer respectively. Generally, mergers and monopolies are viewed as potentially good, and, in fact, necessary for international competition.

"In fact, in order to maintain and improve the international competitiveness of some Canadian industries we may over the next decade require an increase in the number of 'good' mergers, partial mergers and quasi-mergers. . . ."[25] The background report suggests identifying "significant" mergers and determining their "primary" consequences, consequences which might strengthen or create artificial restraints to a *significant degree.* If this is determined, secondary, longrun consideration should be assessed. While the Skeoch and McDonald study is in theoretical and largely ponderous academic language, it provided the philosophical basis for the legal specifics found in the Stage Two Proposals concerning mergers and monopolies.

The criminal penalty for an illegal merger is eliminated largely on the basis of the fact (documented in Chapter 7 in this text) that prosecutions have been difficult and few. Rather than suggesting revisions in methods of policing and/or prosecuting mergers for criminal charges, a civil review is proposed in which the Competition Board would review a select few which "substantially lessen competition." While an earlier version of this bill provided for registration of mergers, it is absent from this bill due to protest from the business community. There was fear review powers being given to the Competition

---

24 Law Reform, *Criminal . . . Action,* p. 41.

25 Lawrence A. Skeoch and Bruce C. McDonald, *Dynamic Change and Accountability in a Canadian Market Economy* (Ottawa: Minister of Supply and Services Canada, 1976).

Board were too broad. Ultimately, it is the Competition Policy Advocate (formerly Director of Investigation and Research) who determines the select few for review. The Competition Board is provided with a number of criteria for making its decision on mergers, although not held to any one of them. Conglomerate mergers are not considered due to the pending investigation by the Royal Commission on Corporate Concentration. The total effect of this merger policy is to place this aspect of the economy under less scrutiny than previously was the case.

Concerning monopolies, the Stage Two Proposals reflect the Skeoch and McDonald judgment that monopolies may be good and necessary. The background report asserts that the standard evils attributed to monopoly—high prices, excessive profits, predatory activities to destroy weaker rivals—are rarely found in monopolies today. Rather, as Machlup notes in his classic work,[26] prices may be temporarily low to eliminate competition. However, Skeoch and McDonald present little data to substantiate these claims about non-effects. In fact, the potential consequences of uneconomical allocation of resources and limited production are neglected.

"In discussing the economic effects of monopolisitic restrictions one should carefully separate the effects on particular groups within the economy from the effect on the economy as a whole. . . . There will always be someone harmed by the restrictions. . . . "[27]

Cy Gonick has pointed out the costs of monopolies in both the United States and Canada:

A U.S. study concludes that the overall cost of monopoly and shared monopoly in terms of lost production is somewhere between $48 billion and $60 billion annually. In Canada, lost output due to the same cause would be in the order of $4.5 to $6 billion dollars. The lost tax revenues alone from this wealth would go a long way towards ending poverty and pollution. The redistribution of income from monopoly profits that transfers income from consumers to shareholders is estimated at $2.3 billion annually in the U.S. and $2 to $3 billion in Canada. Monopolistic firms thus contribute to inequality, inflation and unemployment. Unemployment results since monopolies, as noted, significantly reduce output which in turn reduces the number of workers who would otherwise be producing.[28]

---

26 Fritz Machlup, *The Political Economy of Monopoly* (Baltimore: The Johns Hopkins Press, 1952). For a good collection of recent studies, see Yale Brozen, ed., *The Competitive Economy: Selected Readings* (Morristown, New Jersey: General Learning Press, 1975).

27 Machlup, *Monopoly*, p. 30.

28 C. Gonick, *Inflation or Depression* (Toronto: James Lorimer Co., 1975), p. 22.

Such consequences are not addressed by the background report or the proposed legislation.

In order to further encourage monopolies, specialization agreements are recommended. Groups of companies could apply to the Competition Board to specialize their production, and thus not compete against one another, in order to achieve lower cost output. Whether the lower cost output is to be evident in the consumer price is not addressed. In fact, the entire issue of product price for consumers is hardly mentioned in discussions of "efficiency" and "superior economic performance". As Machlup noted, someone is always harmed by monopolistic restrictions. If this is the case, more adequate protection of consumer interests is needed. The beginning of such interest is provided for through class action suits.

Class Action

For the first time, amendments to the Combines Act, effective January 1, 1976, provided the victim of an anti-competition offence with a civil damages remedy against the offender.[29] While such amendments are important steps in increasing the scope of control and providing more remedies to victims of corporate crime, the second stage revisions of the Combines Act are much more controversial. In particular, the recommendation for class action suits against violators of the Combines Act is proposed in the Stage Two revisions, based upon a report by the Department of Consumer and Corporate Affairs.[30] Generally, the background report concluded that the following benefits will accrue with the use of class action procedures: court time will be more efficiently used by prosecuting one class case, rather than many individual claims; the basic purpose of Combines legislation—efficient allocation of our resources—will be promoted; individuals injured by Combines violations will be provided with a means of redress which minimizes the cost to the complainants; the recovery of class damages will act as an important deterrent to such crime; and profits from such criminal activity will be eliminated.

The report also makes policy recommendations regarding class actions in six areas. It suggests conditions under which class actions may be maintained, procedural safeguards necessary to prevent frivolous claims, safeguards necessary to protect the interests of absent class

29 Civil remedies have long been available in the United States. See Geis, *White Collar Criminal*.

30 Neil J. Williams and Jennifer Whybrow, eds., *A Proposal for Class Actions under Competition Policy Legislation* (Ottawa: Information Canada, 1976).

members, the role of a public official in bringing forth substitute claims where private ones are prohibited, alternate rules covering lawyer's fees and court costs necessary for private class actions, and the merits of consolidating class action cases in the federal court of Canada. These were essentially incorporated into the proposed legislation.

Furthermore, class actions would not be banned only because the plaintiff seeks damages where individual proof of damage may be necessary, and where the claims arise out of different transactions or situations having common questions of fact or law. Also, procedural safeguards are provided to ensure that frivolous and unwarranted actions are not brought against innocent defendants.

Regarding the interests of absent class members, the legislation would allow them to opt out of a class action in order to protect their right to launch an independent suit. In situations where the damage suffered by individual class members is minimal and where the cost of establishing liability and distributing damages is too great, a private class action could be disallowed by the court. Under such circumstances, the Competition Policy Advocate is allowed to bring a substitute class action on behalf of class members. However, the public official could only proceed once a private action had been initiated and rejected by the court. Any reward for damages would be paid over to the federal treasury.

To better enable citizens to bring forward class actions, the ordinary rules with respect to lawyer's fees and court costs would be altered to increase the financial possibility of proceeding with the actions. Generally, no costs will be awarded to either party. There would, however, be certain situations where the defendant could receive his costs. Also, if a class action is successful, reasonable solicitor and client costs will be taken on a *pro rata* basis from compensation awarded to each class member. The class action suit represents a remedy in terms of the power/conflict approach to crime. It is an attempt to shift power from the haves to the have-nots. " . . . class action reflects a concern that individuals in society who do not command economic power and wealth need measures to protect themselves against exploitation by those who do."[31] Besides the general goals of retribution and deterrence, such suits may act as a means of publicizing the nature and extent of criminal corporation behaviour in our society. "Undoubtedly, a large consumer class action has a certain 'showcase' effect, and firms may suffer from the notoriety of having

---

31 Neil J. Williams, "Damages Class Action under the Combines Investigation Act," in *Ibid.*, p. 30.

been accused of injuring a large group of unorganized consumers."[32]
The importance of publicizing corporate crime cannot be overstated.
Given the nature of corporations and their reliance on satisfied
corporate consumers, adverse publicity could be a significant factor if
used in conjunction with the other remedies noted in this chapter.
More effort needs to be placed upon using the mass media to describe
the scope and nature of such crime. In stressing this point, one
criminologist in the United States suggests a "Ten Most Wanted"
white-collar-crime list.[33] By periodically presenting statistical data and
case histories of corporate crime, the public will begin to break down
the artificial distinctions between street and suite crime.

Community Control[34]

Provision should be made by the federal government for local areas to
elect Community and Consumer Councils consisting of 20 members, to
serve for a three year term. Their primary function would be to
examine economic activity which may have a social impact on their
constituents. Specifically, this would include such questions as pollution, employee safety, consumer protection and equal employment
opportunities.

Since many economic activities also have a national impact, provision should be made for linking public participation all the way to the
national level. This could be achieved by Community-Consumer
Councils being established: at the regional level through elections by
the local councils; at the provincial level through elections by the
regional councils; at the national level through elections by provincial
councils.

Through such a mechanism, the average citizen could become
actively involved in the vital economic issues of the day. Issues and
problems developed at the local level could be sent to the next level
for follow up. Each level would be involved in recommending relevant
regulations to the elected officials at the appropriate level of government. Meetings at all levels should be open, with the public and the
press invited to attend and participate. In other words, the meetings

---

32 Jennifer A. Whybrow, "The Case for Class Actions in Canadian Competition
   Policy: An Economist's Viewpoint," in *Ibid.*, p. 210.

33 Geis, "Deterring."

34 This section is adapted from "The Public Interest vs. Concentrated Corporate
   Power," by Ben Carniol, presented to the Royal Commission on Corporate
   Concentration, Calgary, Alberta, 1975. While this brief transcends anticombines
   issues, it is nonetheless quite pertinent.

would be more like public hearings. However, the present practice of public hearings merely going through the motions then acting on their pre-conceived conclusions must cease. Initiatives by individuals and groups in the community should be welcomed.

Economic problems have become too serious to relegate public involvement to an advisory role. The seriousness of the problem has been noted by Peter C. Newman, "No matter how often the politican may proclaim that Canada's economic system spreads abundance among the many, in reality, it creates wealth for the few."[35]

In other words, the public is being hoodwinked into believing there is equal opportunity. Social scientists in the past decade have repeatedly documented the tremendous growth in concentrated power and wealth in the hands of the few. In terms of how the benefits have accrued to the few, the well-known economist, John Kenneth Galbraith, has explained it this way: Corporations will typically not only pass on extra labour costs to the consumer—the price hike will also reflect an increasing profit margin for the corporation.

For the public, the key question becomes: Is the profit margin justifiable, fair and legitimate? What are the social consequences of profits mainly benefitting the very rich as described by Mr. Newman? It is high time the public becomes involved in finding the answers. Some of the answers could be found by the network of Community-Consumer Councils. But often the specific information would be covered up by corporate executives. Therefore, a network of Community-Consumer Tribunals should be established to examine any aspects of corporate activity which may have a social impact on consumers or on the community at large. These Tribunals could be created at the regional, provincial and national levels. They would be appointed for a five-year term by the Community-Consumer Council operating at their level. They would have power to subpoena such individuals and documents as might be necessary for them to discover the facts. Without restricting the generality of the foregoing, their jurisdiction would extend over the following items: corporate hiring and promotion policies with respect to Indians, women, the disabled and other groups suffering discrimination in our society; excessive and wasteful advertising which creates false needs; price collusion by near-monopoly industries; effect of unlimited growth on quality of life; secret deals between big business and public officials; profiteering.

If an economic activity is found by the Tribunal to be against the public interest, the Tribunal would have the power to order an injunc-

---

35 Peter C. Newman, *The Canadian Establishment* (Toronto: McClelland and Stewart, 1975), p. 253.

tion and/or assess damages. If the order of the Tribunal were ignored, the executives and board members of the offending corporations would become liable to heavy fines and/or prison terms. Corporations must be made to serve the public, and not vice versa.

Two Specific Examples

1. Housing: The Central Mortgage and Housing Corporation has estimated that for the 12 largest Canadian cities, 75% of the residential land requirements until 1980 are held by the *six* major developers in each of the regions.[36] That is to say, we have permitted a few giant corporations to corner the market.

2. Food: The food story is hardly better. When there are powerful food chains, how can there be full competition? For example, in Calgary, the Safeway food chain is under a supreme court order of prohibition to prevent it "from engaging in a pricing policy designed to discourage competition and inhibit the growth of small competitors."[37]

From coast to coast, the skyrocketing costs of food and housing have squeezed the aged, the disabled and the unemployed. Not only do the 5 million Canadians who are in poverty feel the pinch, but so do most middle income families who are barely able to make ends meet. The federal wage and price controls will not remedy the situation. The reason is that inflation is primarily caused by the concentraton of power in these and other industries. Until now, that power has not been made accountable to the public.

Provision for public involvement through the proposed councils and tribunals would not only strengthen the quality of participatory democracy throughout Canada, but would also act as a countervailing force against abusive economic practices. It would also prevent substituting a government elite for a corporate elite as the dominant power in the country. Through effective grass-roots participation, community and consumer groups would take on a watch-dog role to ensure that government and economic activities become fully accountable to the public. Therefore, it is unlikely that present government or corporate leaders will endorse effective public participation. However, once the public becomes aware of such alternatives and pushes for their implementation, then the government may have no choice except to bow to the wishes of the public.

---

36 M. Dennis and S. Fish, *Programmes in Search of a Policy* (Toronto: Hakkert, 1972), pp. 323-24.

37 Source: *Report of the Director of Investigation and Research*, Combines Investigation Act (Ottawa: Consumer and Corporate Affairs, March 31, 1974), p. 32.

Corporate Society and the Corporate Citizen

The preceding discussion of social control of the corporate criminal and criminal corporations assumes that the public interest is best served by the current model of the "competitive" marketplace. However, if we come to the conclusion that certain basic social values contribute to both the successful non-criminal corporation and the successful criminal corporation it may be that we pay for our currently socially-prized values. One student of corporate crime in the first decade of this century noted the basic motive behind corporate crime. "They want nothing more than *we all want*—money, power, consideration—in a word, success; but they are in a hurry and are not particular as to their means."[38]

An even earlier observation regarding values and crime is pertinent. "Men may desire superfluities in order to enjoy pleasure unaccompanied with pain, and therefore they commit crimes. The greatest crimes are caused by excess and not by necessity."[39]

In a society where competition, success and material wealth are highly valued, it should not surprise us that the "rules of the game" will often be of less significance than "winning" the game. To understand the implications of criminogenic values for the study of crime in any society is to shed the comforting myth that we can greatly reduce or eliminate criminal behaviour without changing our basic values and life styles.[40] While this does not mean that we will be unable to reduce the magnitude and nature of crime in our society, it does suggest that its persistence is inextricably related to the social fabric. Thus, we may largely get the criminals we deserve. If being a good "corporate citizen"[41] entails pursuing dominant societal values, corporate crime, to some degree, will be with us.

Finally, it is arguable that concentration and monopoly are inevitable and necessary in a capitalist economy.[42] Not only is it in the

---

38 Edward Alsworth Ross, "The Criminaloid," *The Atlantic Monthly*, 99 (January, 1907), p. 46.

39 Aristotle, *Politics*, book II, ch. 7, trans. J. F. C. Welldon (London: MacMillan, 1932), p. 65.

40 Milton L. Barron, "The Criminogenic Society: Social Values and Deviance," in *Current Perspectives on Criminal Behaviour*, ed., Abraham Blumberg (New York: Alfred A. Knopf, 1974), pp. 68-86.

41 John C. Craig, "What is a Good Corporate Citizen?" *The Canadian Review of Sociology and Anthropology*, 11 (August, 1974), pp. 181-96.

42 Ralph Milibrand, *The State in Capitalist Society* (London: The Camelot Press Ltd., 1969). For a discussion of changes in the nature of competition within the context of capitalism which will purportedly help the public, see Milton Moore, *How Much Price Competition? The Prerequisites of an Effective Canadian Competition Policy* (Montreal: McGill-Queen's University Press, 1970).

inherent logic of capitalist history, but without them, Canadian firms could not compete in the export market with the multinational giants. Therefore, the laws are ineffective not only because of the government's lack of interest in pursuing corporate offenders, but also because they are incompatible with an efficient, growth-oriented, internationally competitive capitalism. The recognition of such needs is evident in the Stage Two revisions concerning mergers, monopolies and specialization agreements. The government is proposing essentially that competition should be limited given the needs of our capitalist economy, particularly in terms of the international market place. The implications of this approach are either acceptance of the necessity of both capitalism and the concentration that follows or advocacy of an alternative socioeconomic system.

Index